55 Ice Cream Recipes for Home

By: Kelly Johnson

Table of Contents

- Vanilla Bean Ice Cream
- Chocolate Fudge Brownie Ice Cream
- Strawberry Cheesecake Ice Cream
- Mint Chocolate Chip Ice Cream
- Cookies and Cream Ice Cream
- Butter Pecan Ice Cream
- Pistachio Ice Cream
- Salted Caramel Ice Cream
- Coffee Toffee Crunch Ice Cream
- Rocky Road Ice Cream
- Cherry Garcia Ice Cream (Cherry and Chocolate)
- Coconut Mango Ice Cream
- Peanut Butter Cup Ice Cream
- Raspberry Swirl Ice Cream
- Matcha Green Tea Ice Cream
- Black Sesame Ice Cream
- Lemon Sorbet
- Orange Sherbet
- Pistachio Almond Ice Cream
- Maple Walnut Ice Cream
- Almond Joy Ice Cream (Coconut, Almonds, Chocolate)
- Cinnamon Roll Ice Cream
- Honey Lavender Ice Cream
- Mocha Almond Fudge Ice Cream
- Blueberry Cheesecake Ice Cream
- Tiramisu Ice Cream
- White Chocolate Raspberry Ripple Ice Cream
- Key Lime Pie Ice Cream
- Pomegranate Sorbet
- Avocado Lime Ice Cream
- Dark Chocolate Orange Ice Cream
- Caramelized Banana Ice Cream
- Nutella Swirl Ice Cream
- Balsamic Strawberry Ice Cream
- Red Velvet Ice Cream

- Brown Butter Pecan Ice Cream
- Cardamom Rose Ice Cream
- Earl Grey Tea Ice Cream
- S'mores Ice Cream
- Chocolate Hazelnut Gelato
- Guava Passionfruit Sorbet
- White Chocolate Macadamia Nut Ice Cream
- Raspberry Lemonade Sorbet
- Chocolate Chili Ice Cream
- Blackberry Basil Ice Cream
- Peach Bourbon Ice Cream
- Toasted Coconut Pineapple Ice Cream
- Honey Roasted Fig Ice Cream
- Brown Butter Maple Pecan Ice Cream
- Strawberry Balsamic Swirl Ice Cream
- Chai Tea Latte Ice Cream
- Peanut Butter and Jelly Ice Cream
- Rum Raisin Ice Cream
- Lavender Blueberry Cheesecake Ice Cream
- Coconut Lime Mojito Sorbet

Vanilla Bean Ice Cream

Ingredients:

- 2 cups heavy cream
- 1 cup whole milk
- 3/4 cup granulated sugar
- Pinch of salt
- 1 vanilla bean (or 2 teaspoons pure vanilla extract)
- 6 large egg yolks

Instructions:

1. Prepare the Ice Cream Base:

    In a medium saucepan, combine the heavy cream, whole milk, sugar, and a pinch of salt. Heat the mixture over medium heat, stirring occasionally until it reaches a gentle simmer. Do not boil.
    While the mixture is heating, split the vanilla bean lengthwise and scrape out the seeds using the back of a knife.
    Add the vanilla bean seeds (or vanilla extract) to the milk and cream mixture. If using a vanilla bean, you can also add the scraped pod for additional flavor.
    Once the mixture is hot, remove it from the heat and let it steep for about 30 minutes to allow the vanilla flavor to infuse.

2. Temper the Eggs:

    In a separate bowl, whisk the egg yolks until smooth.
    Gradually whisk a small amount of the hot cream mixture into the egg yolks to temper them. This prevents the eggs from scrambling when added to the hot liquid.
    Gradually whisk the tempered egg mixture back into the saucepan with the remaining hot cream mixture.

3. Cook the Custard:

    Cook the custard over medium heat, stirring continuously with a wooden spoon or heat-resistant spatula. Continue until the mixture thickens and coats the back of the spoon. This should take about 5-7 minutes.
    Remove the custard from heat immediately once thickened.

4. Strain and Chill:

   Strain the custard through a fine-mesh sieve into a clean bowl to remove the vanilla bean pod and any potential cooked egg bits.
   Place the bowl in an ice bath or let it cool at room temperature before covering it with plastic wrap. Chill the custard in the refrigerator for at least 4 hours or preferably overnight.

5. Churn and Freeze:

   Once thoroughly chilled, churn the custard in an ice cream maker according to the manufacturer's instructions.
   Transfer the churned ice cream into a lidded container, pressing a piece of parchment paper directly against the surface of the ice cream to prevent ice crystals from forming.
   Freeze the Vanilla Bean Ice Cream for a few hours or until it reaches your desired consistency.
   Scoop and enjoy!

This Vanilla Bean Ice Cream is rich, creamy, and filled with the pure essence of vanilla. It's a perfect base for topping with your favorite sauces, fruits, or enjoying on its own.

Chocolate Fudge Brownie Ice Cream

Ingredients:

For the Brownies:

- 1/2 cup (1 stick) unsalted butter
- 1 cup granulated sugar
- 2 large eggs
- 1 teaspoon vanilla extract
- 1/3 cup cocoa powder
- 1/2 cup all-purpose flour
- 1/4 teaspoon baking powder
- 1/4 teaspoon salt
- 1/2 cup chocolate chips or chunks

For the Ice Cream Base:

- 2 cups heavy cream
- 1 cup whole milk
- 3/4 cup granulated sugar
- Pinch of salt
- 1 teaspoon vanilla extract

Additional Mix-ins:

- Additional chocolate chips or chunks (optional)

Instructions:

1. Bake the Brownies:

    Preheat your oven to 350°F (175°C). Grease and line an 8x8-inch baking pan with parchment paper.
    In a saucepan, melt the butter over low heat. Remove from heat and stir in the sugar.
    Add the eggs one at a time, beating well after each addition. Stir in the vanilla extract.
    In a separate bowl, sift together cocoa powder, flour, baking powder, and salt.
    Gradually add this dry mixture to the wet ingredients, mixing until just combined.
    Fold in the chocolate chips or chunks.

Pour the brownie batter into the prepared pan and spread it evenly.
Bake for 20-25 minutes or until a toothpick inserted into the center comes out with moist crumbs (not wet batter). Let the brownies cool completely before cutting them into small, bite-sized pieces.

2. Prepare the Ice Cream Base:

In a medium saucepan, combine the heavy cream, whole milk, sugar, and a pinch of salt. Heat the mixture over medium heat, stirring occasionally until it reaches a gentle simmer. Do not boil.
Remove the saucepan from heat and stir in the vanilla extract.
Allow the mixture to cool to room temperature, then cover and refrigerate for at least 4 hours or preferably overnight to let the flavors meld.

3. Churn the Ice Cream:

Once the ice cream base is thoroughly chilled, churn it in an ice cream maker according to the manufacturer's instructions.
During the last few minutes of churning, add the bite-sized brownie pieces and additional chocolate chips if desired.

4. Freeze:

Transfer the churned ice cream into a lidded container, layering it with more brownie pieces and chocolate chips if desired.
Freeze the Chocolate Fudge Brownie Ice Cream for a few hours or until it reaches your preferred consistency.
Scoop into bowls or cones and enjoy the rich and fudgy delight!

This Chocolate Fudge Brownie Ice Cream combines the best of both worlds with creamy chocolate ice cream and chunks of fudgy brownies. It's a heavenly treat for chocolate lovers.

Strawberry Cheesecake Ice Cream

Ingredients:

For the Strawberry Swirl:

- 1 cup fresh strawberries, hulled and diced
- 1/4 cup granulated sugar
- 1 tablespoon lemon juice

For the Cheesecake Base:

- 8 oz (225g) cream cheese, softened
- 1 cup whole milk
- 1 cup heavy cream
- 3/4 cup granulated sugar
- 1 teaspoon vanilla extract
- A pinch of salt

Instructions:

1. Prepare the Strawberry Swirl:

    In a small saucepan, combine diced strawberries, granulated sugar, and lemon juice. Cook over medium heat, stirring occasionally, until the strawberries release their juices and the mixture thickens slightly. This should take about 5-7 minutes.
    Remove from heat and let it cool. Once cooled, blend the mixture until smooth. Set aside.

2. Make the Cheesecake Base:

    In a mixing bowl, beat the softened cream cheese until smooth.
    Add the sugar and continue to beat until well combined and creamy.
    Add the whole milk, heavy cream, vanilla extract, and a pinch of salt. Mix until the mixture is smooth and well incorporated.
    Optionally, you can use a blender to ensure a silky-smooth texture.

3. Combine and Chill:

    Pour the cheesecake base into your ice cream maker and churn according to the manufacturer's instructions.
    During the last few minutes of churning, spoon in dollops of the strawberry swirl, allowing it to mix into the ice cream.

4. Freeze:

> Transfer the churned ice cream into a lidded container, swirling in more of the strawberry mixture if desired.
> Freeze the Strawberry Cheesecake Ice Cream for a few hours or until it reaches your preferred consistency.
> Scoop, serve, and enjoy the delightful combination of creamy cheesecake-flavored ice cream and swirls of sweet strawberry goodness!

This Strawberry Cheesecake Ice Cream is a refreshing and indulgent treat that captures the essence of a classic dessert in frozen form. Enjoy the sweet and tangy flavors in every bite!

Mint Chocolate Chip Ice Cream

Ingredients:

- 2 cups heavy cream
- 1 cup whole milk
- 3/4 cup granulated sugar
- 2 teaspoons peppermint extract
- A few drops of green food coloring (optional)
- 1 cup chocolate chips or chunks (dark or semi-sweet)

Instructions:

1. Prepare the Ice Cream Base:

    In a mixing bowl, whisk together the heavy cream, whole milk, and granulated sugar until the sugar is fully dissolved.
    Add the peppermint extract and green food coloring (if using) to achieve the desired minty flavor and color. Mix well.

2. Chill the Mixture:

    Cover the bowl with plastic wrap and refrigerate the mixture for at least 4 hours or overnight to ensure it's well-chilled.

3. Churn the Ice Cream:

    Once chilled, pour the mixture into your ice cream maker and churn according to the manufacturer's instructions.
    During the last few minutes of churning, add in the chocolate chips or chunks, allowing them to mix evenly into the ice cream.

4. Freeze:

    Transfer the churned Mint Chocolate Chip Ice Cream into a lidded container.
    Optionally, sprinkle additional chocolate chips on top for extra indulgence.
    Freeze the ice cream for a few hours or until it reaches your desired consistency.

5. Scoop and Enjoy:

    Scoop the Mint Chocolate Chip Ice Cream into bowls or cones.
    Garnish with fresh mint leaves or additional chocolate chips if desired.
    Delight in the minty freshness and chocolatey goodness of this homemade ice cream!

This Mint Chocolate Chip Ice Cream is a classic favorite, perfect for cooling down on a warm day or satisfying your sweet tooth with its refreshing and creamy texture. Enjoy the delightful combination of mint and chocolate in every bite!

Cookies and Cream Ice Cream

Ingredients:

For the Ice Cream Base:

- 2 cups heavy cream
- 1 cup whole milk
- 3/4 cup granulated sugar
- 1 teaspoon vanilla extract

For the Cookie Crumbs:

- 20 chocolate sandwich cookies (like Oreo), crushed

Instructions:

1. Prepare the Ice Cream Base:

    In a mixing bowl, whisk together the heavy cream, whole milk, granulated sugar, and vanilla extract until the sugar is fully dissolved.

2. Chill the Mixture:

    Cover the bowl with plastic wrap and refrigerate the mixture for at least 4 hours or overnight to ensure it's well-chilled.

3. Churn the Ice Cream:

    Once chilled, pour the mixture into your ice cream maker and churn according to the manufacturer's instructions.
    During the last few minutes of churning, add in the crushed chocolate sandwich cookies. Let them mix evenly into the ice cream.

4. Freeze:

    Transfer the churned Cookies and Cream Ice Cream into a lidded container.
    Optionally, sprinkle additional cookie crumbs on top for extra texture.
    Freeze the ice cream for a few hours or until it reaches your desired consistency.

5. Scoop and Enjoy:

    Scoop the Cookies and Cream Ice Cream into bowls or cones.
    Indulge in the delightful combination of creamy vanilla ice cream with crunchy chocolate cookie bits.

Serve and savor the classic taste of this beloved ice cream flavor!

This Cookies and Cream Ice Cream is a crowd-pleaser, combining the richness of vanilla with the crunch of chocolate cookies. It's perfect for any occasion and sure to be a hit with both kids and adults alike. Enjoy every spoonful of this delightful treat!

Butter Pecan Ice Cream

Ingredients:

For the Butter Pecans:

- 1 cup pecans, chopped
- 2 tablespoons unsalted butter
- Pinch of salt

For the Ice Cream Base:

- 2 cups heavy cream
- 1 cup whole milk
- 3/4 cup granulated sugar
- 1 teaspoon vanilla extract

Instructions:

1. Prepare the Butter Pecans:

    In a skillet over medium heat, melt the butter.
    Add the chopped pecans and a pinch of salt. Toast the pecans in the butter, stirring frequently, until they become fragrant and slightly browned. Be careful not to burn them. Remove the buttered pecans from heat and let them cool.

2. Prepare the Ice Cream Base:

    In a mixing bowl, whisk together the heavy cream, whole milk, granulated sugar, and vanilla extract until the sugar is fully dissolved.

3. Chill the Mixture:

    Cover the bowl with plastic wrap and refrigerate the mixture for at least 4 hours or overnight to ensure it's well-chilled.

4. Churn the Ice Cream:

    Once chilled, pour the mixture into your ice cream maker and churn according to the manufacturer's instructions.
    During the last few minutes of churning, add in the cooled buttered pecans. Let them mix evenly into the ice cream.

5. Freeze:

Transfer the churned Butter Pecan Ice Cream into a lidded container.
Optionally, sprinkle additional chopped pecans on top for extra crunch.
Freeze the ice cream for a few hours or until it reaches your desired consistency.

6. Scoop and Enjoy:

Scoop the Butter Pecan Ice Cream into bowls or cones.
Delight in the creamy texture and nutty flavor of this classic homemade treat.
Serve and enjoy the buttery goodness of Butter Pecan Ice Cream!

This Butter Pecan Ice Cream is a delightful combination of smooth, buttery ice cream and crunchy, toasted pecans. It's a timeless favorite that's perfect for satisfying your sweet cravings. Enjoy every spoonful!

Pistachio Ice Cream

Ingredients:

- 1 cup shelled pistachios, unsalted
- 2 cups heavy cream
- 1 cup whole milk
- 3/4 cup granulated sugar
- 1 teaspoon almond extract
- Green food coloring (optional, for color)

Instructions:

1. Prepare the Pistachios:

    In a food processor, pulse the pistachios until finely chopped. You can leave some larger pieces for added texture if desired.
    In a skillet over medium heat, toast the chopped pistachios for a few minutes until they become fragrant. Be cautious not to burn them. Set aside to cool.

2. Make the Pistachio Paste:

    Transfer half of the chopped pistachios to the food processor and blend until it forms a smooth paste. Add a bit of the heavy cream if needed to help with the blending.
    Combine the pistachio paste with the remaining chopped pistachios. This creates a textured base for the ice cream.

3. Prepare the Ice Cream Base:

    In a mixing bowl, whisk together the heavy cream, whole milk, granulated sugar, and almond extract until the sugar is fully dissolved.
    Add the pistachio mixture to the ice cream base and mix well. Add green food coloring if you desire a more vibrant color.

4. Chill the Mixture:

    Cover the bowl with plastic wrap and refrigerate the mixture for at least 4 hours or overnight to ensure it's well-chilled.

5. Churn the Ice Cream:

    Once chilled, pour the mixture into your ice cream maker and churn according to the manufacturer's instructions.

During the last few minutes of churning, add any additional chopped pistachios for extra crunch.

6. Freeze:

Transfer the churned Pistachio Ice Cream into a lidded container.
Freeze the ice cream for a few hours or until it reaches your desired consistency.

7. Scoop and Enjoy:

Scoop the Pistachio Ice Cream into bowls or cones.
Delight in the nutty and creamy flavor of this homemade treat.
Serve and savor the unique taste of Pistachio Ice Cream!

This Pistachio Ice Cream is a delightful dessert that showcases the distinct flavor of pistachios. It's a perfect treat for those who appreciate the rich and nutty taste of this unique ice cream flavor. Enjoy!

Salted Caramel Ice Cream

Ingredients:

For the Caramel Sauce:

- 1 cup granulated sugar
- 6 tablespoons unsalted butter, cut into pieces
- 1/2 cup heavy cream
- 1 teaspoon sea salt (adjust to taste)

For the Ice Cream Base:

- 2 cups heavy cream
- 1 cup whole milk
- 3/4 cup granulated sugar
- 1 teaspoon vanilla extract

Instructions:

1. Make the Caramel Sauce:

   In a heavy saucepan, heat granulated sugar over medium heat. Stir constantly with a heat-resistant spatula or wooden spoon until the sugar melts and turns amber in color. Add the butter to the melted sugar and stir until the butter is fully melted.
   Slowly pour in the heavy cream while stirring constantly. Be cautious as the mixture will bubble up.
   Continue to cook and stir until the caramel is smooth. Remove from heat and stir in the sea salt. Allow the caramel sauce to cool.

2. Prepare the Ice Cream Base:

   In a mixing bowl, whisk together the heavy cream, whole milk, granulated sugar, and vanilla extract until the sugar is fully dissolved.
   Add a portion of the caramel sauce to the ice cream base and mix well. Reserve some caramel sauce for layering or drizzling on top.

3. Chill the Mixture:

   Cover the bowl with plastic wrap and refrigerate the mixture for at least 4 hours or overnight to ensure it's well-chilled.

4. Churn the Ice Cream:

Once chilled, pour the mixture into your ice cream maker and churn according to the manufacturer's instructions.

During the last few minutes of churning, drizzle in more of the reserved caramel sauce to create swirls in the ice cream.

5. Freeze:

   Transfer the churned Salted Caramel Ice Cream into a lidded container.

   Optionally, drizzle additional caramel sauce on top before freezing.

   Freeze the ice cream for a few hours or until it reaches your desired consistency.

6. Scoop and Enjoy:

   Scoop the Salted Caramel Ice Cream into bowls or cones.

   Delight in the sweet and salty combination of flavors in every spoonful.

   Serve and savor the rich and indulgent taste of Salted Caramel Ice Cream!

This Salted Caramel Ice Cream is a luxurious treat with the perfect blend of sweetness and a hint of sea salt. It's sure to become a favorite for caramel lovers. Enjoy the creamy goodness!

Coffee Toffee Crunch Ice Cream

Ingredients:

For the Coffee Toffee Crunch:

- 1/2 cup coarsely ground coffee beans (for steeping)
- 1 cup heavy cream
- 1 cup whole milk
- 3/4 cup granulated sugar
- 1 teaspoon vanilla extract
- 1/2 cup toffee bits or crushed toffee candies

Instructions:

1. Prepare the Coffee Infusion:

    In a saucepan, combine coarsely ground coffee beans, heavy cream, and whole milk. Heat the mixture over medium heat until it just begins to simmer. Do not let it boil. Remove the saucepan from heat and let the coffee steep in the mixture for about 30 minutes.
    Strain the mixture through a fine-mesh sieve to remove the coffee grounds.

2. Make the Ice Cream Base:

    In a mixing bowl, whisk together the strained coffee-infused cream, granulated sugar, and vanilla extract until the sugar is fully dissolved.
    Add the toffee bits or crushed toffee candies to the mixture and stir well.

3. Chill the Mixture:

    Cover the bowl with plastic wrap and refrigerate the mixture for at least 4 hours or overnight to ensure it's well-chilled.

4. Churn the Ice Cream:

    Once chilled, pour the mixture into your ice cream maker and churn according to the manufacturer's instructions.
    During the last few minutes of churning, add extra toffee bits for added crunch.

5. Freeze:

    Transfer the churned Coffee Toffee Crunch Ice Cream into a lidded container.
    Optionally, sprinkle additional toffee bits on top before freezing.

Freeze the ice cream for a few hours or until it reaches your desired consistency.

6. Scoop and Enjoy:

> Scoop the Coffee Toffee Crunch Ice Cream into bowls or cones.
> Delight in the rich coffee flavor and the delightful crunch of toffee in every bite.
> Serve and savor the deliciousness of this homemade treat!

This Coffee Toffee Crunch Ice Cream is a delightful blend of creamy coffee goodness and the satisfying crunch of toffee. It's the perfect treat for coffee lovers and those who enjoy a bit of crunch in their ice cream. Enjoy every spoonful!

Rocky Road Ice Cream

Ingredients:

For the Chocolate Ice Cream Base:

- 2 cups heavy cream
- 1 cup whole milk
- 3/4 cup granulated sugar
- 1/2 cup unsweetened cocoa powder
- 1 teaspoon vanilla extract

For the Rocky Road Mix-ins:

- 1 cup mini marshmallows
- 1 cup chopped nuts (walnuts or almonds)
- 1/2 cup chocolate chips or chunks

Instructions:

1. Prepare the Chocolate Ice Cream Base:

    In a mixing bowl, whisk together the heavy cream, whole milk, granulated sugar, cocoa powder, and vanilla extract until the sugar is fully dissolved.
    Ensure that the cocoa powder is well incorporated to achieve a smooth chocolate base.

2. Chill the Mixture:

    Cover the bowl with plastic wrap and refrigerate the mixture for at least 4 hours or overnight to ensure it's well-chilled.

3. Churn the Ice Cream:

    Once chilled, pour the mixture into your ice cream maker and churn according to the manufacturer's instructions.
    During the last few minutes of churning, add the mini marshmallows, chopped nuts, and chocolate chips. Let them mix evenly into the ice cream.

4. Freeze:

    Transfer the churned Rocky Road Ice Cream into a lidded container.
    Optionally, sprinkle additional marshmallows, nuts, and chocolate chips on top for extra indulgence.
    Freeze the ice cream for a few hours or until it reaches your desired consistency.

5. Scoop and Enjoy:

> Scoop the Rocky Road Ice Cream into bowls or cones.
> Delight in the rich chocolate flavor, the crunch of nuts, and the gooey goodness of marshmallows in every spoonful.
> Serve and savor the classic taste of this beloved ice cream flavor!

This Rocky Road Ice Cream is a crowd-pleaser with its perfect combination of textures and flavors. It's a timeless treat that's sure to bring joy to chocolate and nut enthusiasts. Enjoy the deliciousness!

Cherry Garcia Ice Cream (Cherry and Chocolate)

Ingredients:

For the Cherry Base:

- 2 cups fresh or frozen cherries, pitted and halved
- 1/2 cup granulated sugar
- 1 tablespoon lemon juice

For the Chocolate Ice Cream Base:

- 2 cups heavy cream
- 1 cup whole milk
- 3/4 cup granulated sugar
- 1/2 cup unsweetened cocoa powder
- 1 teaspoon vanilla extract

For the Chocolate Chunks:

- 1/2 cup chocolate chunks or chocolate chips

Instructions:

1. Prepare the Cherry Base:

    In a saucepan, combine the pitted and halved cherries, granulated sugar, and lemon juice.
    Cook over medium heat until the cherries release their juices and the sugar dissolves, creating a syrupy consistency.
    Remove from heat and let the cherry mixture cool.

2. Make the Chocolate Ice Cream Base:

    In a mixing bowl, whisk together the heavy cream, whole milk, granulated sugar, cocoa powder, and vanilla extract until the sugar is fully dissolved.
    Ensure that the cocoa powder is well incorporated to achieve a smooth chocolate base.

3. Combine the Bases:

    Once the cherry mixture has cooled, fold it into the chocolate ice cream base. Mix gently to create swirls of cherry throughout the ice cream.
    Add the chocolate chunks or chips and stir to distribute them evenly.

4. Chill the Mixture:

    Cover the bowl with plastic wrap and refrigerate the mixture for at least 4 hours or overnight to ensure it's well-chilled.

5. Churn the Ice Cream:

    Once chilled, pour the mixture into your ice cream maker and churn according to the manufacturer's instructions.
    During the last few minutes of churning, add extra chocolate chunks for added richness.

6. Freeze:

    Transfer the churned Cherry Garcia Ice Cream into a lidded container.
    Optionally, sprinkle additional chocolate chunks on top before freezing.
    Freeze the ice cream for a few hours or until it reaches your desired consistency.

7. Scoop and Enjoy:

    Scoop the Cherry Garcia Ice Cream into bowls or cones.
    Delight in the fruity sweetness of cherries, the richness of chocolate, and the creaminess of this classic Ben & Jerry's-inspired flavor.
    Serve and savor the deliciousness of homemade Cherry Garcia Ice Cream!

This Cherry Garcia Ice Cream is a wonderful blend of fruity and chocolatey goodness, capturing the essence of the beloved commercial flavor. Enjoy this homemade treat with the perfect balance of flavors!

Coconut Mango Ice Cream

Ingredients:

- 2 cups fresh or frozen mango chunks
- 1 can (14 ounces) coconut milk
- 1 cup coconut cream
- 1/2 cup granulated sugar
- 1 teaspoon vanilla extract
- 1 tablespoon lime juice (optional, for a hint of citrus)

Instructions:

1. Prepare the Mango Puree:

    In a blender or food processor, puree the mango chunks until smooth. Set aside.

2. Make the Ice Cream Base:

    In a mixing bowl, whisk together the coconut milk, coconut cream, granulated sugar, vanilla extract, and lime juice (if using) until the sugar is fully dissolved.
    Add the mango puree to the coconut mixture and stir well to combine.

3. Chill the Mixture:

    Cover the bowl with plastic wrap and refrigerate the mixture for at least 4 hours or overnight to ensure it's well-chilled.

4. Churn the Ice Cream:

    Once chilled, pour the mixture into your ice cream maker and churn according to the manufacturer's instructions.

5. Freeze:

    Transfer the churned Coconut Mango Ice Cream into a lidded container.
    Optionally, garnish with shredded coconut or additional mango chunks on top before freezing.
    Freeze the ice cream for a few hours or until it reaches your desired consistency.

6. Scoop and Enjoy:

    Scoop the Coconut Mango Ice Cream into bowls or cones.
    Delight in the tropical fusion of coconut and mango in every spoonful.

Serve and savor the exotic taste of this homemade Coconut Mango Ice Cream!

This Coconut Mango Ice Cream is a delightful treat that captures the essence of a tropical paradise. It's a perfect choice for those hot summer days when you crave a refreshing and fruity ice cream. Enjoy the tropical bliss!

Peanut Butter Cup Ice Cream

Ingredients:

For the Peanut Butter Ice Cream Base:

- 2 cups heavy cream
- 1 cup whole milk
- 3/4 cup granulated sugar
- 1/2 cup creamy peanut butter
- 1 teaspoon vanilla extract

For the Peanut Butter Cups Mix-ins:

- 1 cup chopped peanut butter cups (or mini peanut butter cups)

Instructions:

1. Make the Peanut Butter Ice Cream Base:

    In a mixing bowl, whisk together the heavy cream, whole milk, granulated sugar, peanut butter, and vanilla extract until the sugar is fully dissolved and the peanut butter is well incorporated.
    Ensure that the peanut butter is evenly distributed to achieve a smooth and creamy base.

2. Chill the Mixture:

    Cover the bowl with plastic wrap and refrigerate the mixture for at least 4 hours or overnight to ensure it's well-chilled.

3. Churn the Ice Cream:

    Once chilled, pour the mixture into your ice cream maker and churn according to the manufacturer's instructions.
    During the last few minutes of churning, add the chopped peanut butter cups to distribute them evenly into the ice cream.

4. Freeze:

    Transfer the churned Peanut Butter Cup Ice Cream into a lidded container.
    Optionally, sprinkle additional chopped peanut butter cups on top for extra indulgence.
    Freeze the ice cream for a few hours or until it reaches your desired consistency.

5. Scoop and Enjoy:

Scoop the Peanut Butter Cup Ice Cream into bowls or cones.
Delight in the creamy peanut butter flavor and the irresistible chunks of chocolate and peanut butter cups in every bite.
Serve and savor the deliciousness of this homemade Peanut Butter Cup Ice Cream!

This Peanut Butter Cup Ice Cream is a dream come true for peanut butter and chocolate lovers. It's a decadent and satisfying treat that captures the essence of the classic candy. Enjoy the creamy, nutty goodness!

Raspberry Swirl Ice Cream

Ingredients:

For the Raspberry Swirl:

- 2 cups fresh or frozen raspberries
- 1/2 cup granulated sugar
- 1 tablespoon lemon juice

For the Ice Cream Base:

- 2 cups heavy cream
- 1 cup whole milk
- 3/4 cup granulated sugar
- 1 teaspoon vanilla extract

Instructions:

1. Prepare the Raspberry Swirl:

    In a saucepan, combine the raspberries, granulated sugar, and lemon juice. Cook over medium heat until the raspberries break down and the sugar dissolves, creating a thick raspberry sauce.
    Remove from heat and strain the mixture through a fine-mesh sieve to remove the seeds. Allow the raspberry sauce to cool.

2. Make the Ice Cream Base:

    In a mixing bowl, whisk together the heavy cream, whole milk, granulated sugar, and vanilla extract until the sugar is fully dissolved.

3. Combine the Swirl and Base:

    Once the raspberry sauce has cooled, gently fold it into the ice cream base. Mix just enough to create swirls of raspberry throughout the ice cream.

4. Chill the Mixture:

    Cover the bowl with plastic wrap and refrigerate the mixture for at least 4 hours or overnight to ensure it's well-chilled.

5. Churn the Ice Cream:

Once chilled, pour the mixture into your ice cream maker and churn according to the manufacturer's instructions.

6. Freeze:

    Transfer the churned Raspberry Swirl Ice Cream into a lidded container.
    Optionally, drizzle additional raspberry sauce on top or create more swirls with a spoon.
    Freeze the ice cream for a few hours or until it reaches your desired consistency.

7. Scoop and Enjoy:

    Scoop the Raspberry Swirl Ice Cream into bowls or cones.
    Delight in the vibrant flavor of tart raspberries and the smoothness of the creamy ice cream.
    Serve and savor the refreshing taste of this homemade Raspberry Swirl Ice Cream!

This Raspberry Swirl Ice Cream is a burst of fruity goodness with the perfect balance of sweet and tart. It's a delightful treat for those who love the bright flavor of raspberries. Enjoy the refreshing swirls!

Matcha Green Tea Ice Cream

Ingredients:

- 2 cups heavy cream
- 1 cup whole milk
- 3/4 cup granulated sugar
- 3 tablespoons high-quality matcha powder
- 1 teaspoon vanilla extract

Instructions:

1. Prepare the Matcha Mixture:

    In a mixing bowl, whisk together the matcha powder and a small amount of the whole milk to create a smooth paste.
    Gradually add the remaining whole milk and continue whisking until the matcha is fully dissolved.

2. Make the Ice Cream Base:

    In a separate mixing bowl, whisk together the heavy cream, granulated sugar, and vanilla extract until the sugar is fully dissolved.
    Add the matcha mixture to the cream mixture and whisk until well combined.

3. Chill the Mixture:

    Cover the bowl with plastic wrap and refrigerate the mixture for at least 4 hours or overnight to ensure it's well-chilled.

4. Churn the Ice Cream:

    Once chilled, pour the mixture into your ice cream maker and churn according to the manufacturer's instructions.

5. Freeze:

    Transfer the churned Matcha Green Tea Ice Cream into a lidded container. Optionally, sprinkle additional matcha powder on top or create swirls with a spoon.
    Freeze the ice cream for a few hours or until it reaches your desired consistency.

6. Scoop and Enjoy:

Scoop the Matcha Green Tea Ice Cream into bowls or cones.
Delight in the distinct and robust flavor of matcha in every creamy bite.
Serve and savor the unique taste of this homemade Matcha Green Tea Ice Cream!

This Matcha Green Tea Ice Cream is a refreshing and sophisticated treat for matcha enthusiasts. It combines the rich creaminess of ice cream with the bold and earthy notes of high-quality matcha powder. Enjoy the elegance of matcha in dessert form!

Black Sesame Ice Cream

Ingredients:

- 2 cups heavy cream
- 1 cup whole milk
- 3/4 cup granulated sugar
- 1/2 cup black sesame seeds
- 1 teaspoon black sesame paste (optional, for intensified flavor)
- 1 teaspoon vanilla extract

Instructions:

1. Toast the Black Sesame Seeds:

    In a dry skillet over medium heat, toast the black sesame seeds until fragrant. Be careful not to burn them.
    Allow the toasted sesame seeds to cool.

2. Grind the Sesame Seeds:

    Grind the cooled black sesame seeds in a food processor or blender until they form a coarse powder. You can leave some texture for added crunch, or grind them finer for a smoother consistency.

3. Make the Black Sesame Paste (Optional):

    If using black sesame paste, mix it with a small amount of whole milk to create a smooth paste.

4. Prepare the Ice Cream Base:

    In a mixing bowl, whisk together the heavy cream, whole milk, granulated sugar, ground black sesame seeds, black sesame paste (if using), and vanilla extract until the sugar is fully dissolved.

5. Chill the Mixture:

    Cover the bowl with plastic wrap and refrigerate the mixture for at least 4 hours or overnight to ensure it's well-chilled.

6. Churn the Ice Cream:

Once chilled, pour the mixture into your ice cream maker and churn according to the manufacturer's instructions.

7. Freeze:

Transfer the churned Black Sesame Ice Cream into a lidded container.
Optionally, sprinkle additional ground black sesame seeds on top for added texture.
Freeze the ice cream for a few hours or until it reaches your desired consistency.

8. Scoop and Enjoy:

Scoop the Black Sesame Ice Cream into bowls or cones.
Relish in the rich and nutty flavor of black sesame with each creamy bite.
Serve and savor the unique taste of this homemade Black Sesame Ice Cream!

This Black Sesame Ice Cream is a sophisticated and delightful dessert, offering a distinct nuttiness and a beautiful charcoal hue. It's a perfect choice for those who appreciate the unique and exotic flavors of black sesame. Enjoy the indulgence!

Lemon Sorbet

Ingredients:

- 1 cup fresh lemon juice (from about 6-8 lemons)
- 1 cup granulated sugar
- 2 cups water
- Zest of 1-2 lemons (optional, for extra flavor)

Instructions:

1. Prepare the Lemon Syrup:

    In a saucepan, combine the granulated sugar and water over medium heat.
    Stir until the sugar dissolves completely, creating a simple syrup.
    Remove the saucepan from heat and let the syrup cool to room temperature.

2. Extract Lemon Juice:

    Squeeze enough lemons to obtain 1 cup of fresh lemon juice.
    If desired, zest 1-2 lemons to add extra citrus flavor to the sorbet.

3. Combine and Chill:

    In a mixing bowl, combine the lemon juice and the cooled simple syrup.
    Add the lemon zest if using.
    Mix well to ensure the flavors are evenly distributed.
    Cover the bowl with plastic wrap and refrigerate the mixture for at least 4 hours or overnight.

4. Freeze:

    Pour the chilled lemon mixture into an ice cream maker and churn according to the manufacturer's instructions.

5. Serve:

    Transfer the churned Lemon Sorbet into a lidded container.
    Freeze for an additional few hours or until it reaches your desired consistency.

6. Scoop and Enjoy:

    Scoop the Lemon Sorbet into bowls or cones.

Relish in the zesty and refreshing flavor of homemade Lemon Sorbet. Serve and enjoy this delightful frozen treat!

This Lemon Sorbet is a perfect palate cleanser and a light, refreshing dessert. The bright and citrusy notes make it a wonderful choice for hot summer days or as a palate cleanser between courses. Enjoy the burst of lemony goodness!

Orange Sherbet

Ingredients:

- 1 cup fresh orange juice (from about 4-6 oranges)
- 1 cup granulated sugar
- 2 cups whole milk
- Zest of 1 orange (optional, for extra flavor)
- 1 teaspoon vanilla extract

Instructions:

1. Prepare the Orange Syrup:

    In a saucepan, combine the granulated sugar and a half cup of orange juice over medium heat.
    Stir until the sugar dissolves completely, creating a simple syrup.
    Remove the saucepan from heat and let the syrup cool to room temperature.

2. Extract Orange Juice:

    Squeeze enough oranges to obtain 1 cup of fresh orange juice.
    If desired, zest 1 orange to enhance the orange flavor in the sherbet.

3. Combine and Chill:

    In a mixing bowl, combine the remaining orange juice, whole milk, vanilla extract, and the cooled orange syrup.
    Add the orange zest if using.
    Mix well to ensure the flavors are evenly distributed.
    Cover the bowl with plastic wrap and refrigerate the mixture for at least 4 hours or overnight.

4. Freeze:

    Pour the chilled orange mixture into an ice cream maker and churn according to the manufacturer's instructions.

5. Serve:

    Transfer the churned Orange Sherbet into a lidded container.
    Freeze for an additional few hours or until it reaches your desired consistency.

6. Scoop and Enjoy:

    Scoop the Orange Sherbet into bowls or cones.
    Delight in the citrusy and creamy goodness of homemade Orange Sherbet.
    Serve and enjoy this refreshing frozen treat!

This Orange Sherbet is a delightful combination of citrusy orange flavor and creamy texture. It's a perfect choice for those who love the tanginess of oranges in a frozen dessert. Enjoy the cool and zesty sensation!

Pistachio Almond Ice Cream

Ingredients:

- 1 cup shelled pistachios
- 1 cup almonds, blanched and peeled
- 1 cup granulated sugar
- 2 cups heavy cream
- 1 cup whole milk
- 1 teaspoon almond extract
- Green food coloring (optional, for a vibrant pistachio color)

Instructions:

1. Prepare the Nut Mixture:

    In a food processor, combine the shelled pistachios and blanched almonds. Pulse the nuts until they form a coarse meal. Be careful not to over-process, as you want some texture in the ice cream.

2. Make the Nut Paste:

    Add 1/2 cup of the granulated sugar to the nut mixture in the food processor. Continue processing until the nuts and sugar combine into a thick paste. Set aside.

3. Prepare the Ice Cream Base:

    In a mixing bowl, whisk together the heavy cream, whole milk, and the remaining 1/2 cup of granulated sugar until the sugar is fully dissolved.
    Add the almond extract and mix well.
    If desired, add a few drops of green food coloring for a vibrant pistachio color.

4. Combine Nut Paste and Ice Cream Base:

    Gently fold the nut paste into the ice cream base, ensuring even distribution.

5. Chill the Mixture:

    Cover the bowl with plastic wrap and refrigerate the mixture for at least 4 hours or overnight to ensure it's well-chilled.

6. Freeze:

Pour the chilled pistachio almond mixture into an ice cream maker and churn according to the manufacturer's instructions.

7. Serve:

    Transfer the churned Pistachio Almond Ice Cream into a lidded container.
    Freeze for an additional few hours or until it reaches your desired consistency.

8. Scoop and Enjoy:

    Scoop the Pistachio Almond Ice Cream into bowls or cones.
    Delight in the nutty and creamy goodness of homemade Pistachio Almond Ice Cream.
    Serve and savor the unique flavor of this delightful frozen treat!

This Pistachio Almond Ice Cream combines the distinct flavors of pistachios and almonds for a rich and nutty dessert experience. It's a perfect choice for those who enjoy the delightful crunch and flavor of nuts in their ice cream. Enjoy the decadence!

Maple Walnut Ice Cream

Ingredients:

- 1 cup chopped walnuts
- 1 cup pure maple syrup
- 2 cups heavy cream
- 1 cup whole milk
- 3/4 cup granulated sugar
- 1 teaspoon vanilla extract

Instructions:

1. Toast the Walnuts:

    In a dry skillet over medium heat, toast the chopped walnuts until they become fragrant. Be careful not to burn them. Set aside to cool.

2. Prepare the Maple Syrup:

    In a saucepan, warm the pure maple syrup over low heat just until it's heated through. Remove from heat and let it cool to room temperature.

3. Make the Ice Cream Base:

    In a mixing bowl, whisk together the heavy cream, whole milk, granulated sugar, and vanilla extract until the sugar is fully dissolved.
    Add the cooled maple syrup to the cream mixture and whisk until well combined.

4. Chill the Mixture:

    Cover the bowl with plastic wrap and refrigerate the mixture for at least 4 hours or overnight to ensure it's well-chilled.

5. Freeze:

    Pour the chilled maple walnut mixture into an ice cream maker and churn according to the manufacturer's instructions.

6. Add Walnuts:

    During the last few minutes of churning, add the toasted chopped walnuts to the ice cream maker, allowing them to evenly mix into the ice cream.

7. Serve:

>   Transfer the churned Maple Walnut Ice Cream into a lidded container.
>   Freeze for an additional few hours or until it reaches your desired consistency.

8. Scoop and Enjoy:

>   Scoop the Maple Walnut Ice Cream into bowls or cones.
>   Relish in the comforting and nutty flavors of homemade Maple Walnut Ice Cream.
>   Serve and enjoy this delightful frozen treat!

This Maple Walnut Ice Cream offers the rich sweetness of pure maple syrup combined with the crunch of toasted walnuts. It's a cozy and indulgent ice cream that captures the essence of fall. Enjoy the warmth and flavor!

Almond Joy Ice Cream (Coconut, Almonds, Chocolate)

Ingredients:

- 1 cup shredded coconut (sweetened or unsweetened, based on preference)
- 1 cup chopped almonds
- 2 cups heavy cream
- 1 cup whole milk
- 3/4 cup granulated sugar
- 1 teaspoon coconut extract
- 1/2 cup chocolate chips or chopped chocolate

Instructions:

1. Toast Coconut and Almonds:

    In a dry skillet over medium heat, toast the shredded coconut until it turns golden brown. Stir frequently to prevent burning.
    In the same skillet, toast the chopped almonds until they are lightly browned and fragrant. Set aside to cool.

2. Make the Ice Cream Base:

    In a mixing bowl, whisk together the heavy cream, whole milk, granulated sugar, and coconut extract until the sugar is fully dissolved.

3. Add Coconut and Almonds:

    Add the toasted shredded coconut and chopped almonds to the ice cream base. Mix well to ensure even distribution.

4. Chill the Mixture:

    Cover the bowl with plastic wrap and refrigerate the mixture for at least 4 hours or overnight to ensure it's well-chilled.

5. Freeze:

    Pour the chilled Almond Joy mixture into an ice cream maker and churn according to the manufacturer's instructions.

6. Add Chocolate:

During the last few minutes of churning, add the chocolate chips or chopped chocolate to the ice cream maker, allowing them to evenly mix into the ice cream.

7. Serve:

Transfer the churned Almond Joy Ice Cream into a lidded container.
Freeze for an additional few hours or until it reaches your desired consistency.

8. Scoop and Enjoy:

Scoop the Almond Joy Ice Cream into bowls or cones.
Delight in the tropical and chocolatey flavors of homemade Almond Joy Ice Cream.
Serve and enjoy this decadent frozen treat!

This Almond Joy Ice Cream brings together the classic combination of coconut, almonds, and chocolate in a cool and creamy dessert. It's a delightful treat that captures the essence of the popular candy bar. Indulge in the tropical goodness!

Cinnamon Roll Ice Cream

Ingredients:

For the Cinnamon Roll Swirl:

- 1/4 cup unsalted butter, melted
- 1/4 cup brown sugar, packed
- 1 tablespoon ground cinnamon

For the Ice Cream Base:

- 2 cups heavy cream
- 1 cup whole milk
- 3/4 cup granulated sugar
- 1 teaspoon vanilla extract

Optional Add-ins:

- 1/2 cup crushed cinnamon roll pieces (from store-bought or homemade cinnamon rolls)
- Cream cheese frosting for swirling (homemade or store-bought)

Instructions:

1. Prepare the Cinnamon Roll Swirl:

    In a small bowl, mix together the melted butter, brown sugar, and ground cinnamon to create the cinnamon roll swirl. Set aside.

2. Make the Ice Cream Base:

    In a mixing bowl, whisk together the heavy cream, whole milk, granulated sugar, and vanilla extract until the sugar is fully dissolved.

3. Add Cinnamon Roll Swirl:

    Pour a small amount of the ice cream base into the ice cream maker.
    Drizzle some of the cinnamon roll swirl over the ice cream base.
    Repeat the process, layering the ice cream base and cinnamon roll swirl until both are used up.

4. Freeze:

    Pour the layered mixture into the ice cream maker and churn according to the manufacturer's instructions.

5. Optional Add-ins:

> During the last few minutes of churning, add the crushed cinnamon roll pieces to the ice cream maker, allowing them to evenly mix into the ice cream.
> If desired, swirl in cream cheese frosting for added richness and flavor.

6. Serve:

> Transfer the churned Cinnamon Roll Ice Cream into a lidded container.
> Freeze for an additional few hours or until it reaches your desired consistency.

7. Scoop and Enjoy:

> Scoop the Cinnamon Roll Ice Cream into bowls or cones.
> Delight in the sweet and spiced flavors of homemade Cinnamon Roll Ice Cream.
> Serve and enjoy this delicious frozen treat reminiscent of your favorite cinnamon roll!

This Cinnamon Roll Ice Cream captures the essence of cinnamon rolls with swirls of cinnamon, brown sugar, and optional cream cheese frosting. It's a delightful frozen dessert that brings the warmth and comfort of cinnamon rolls to your ice cream bowl. Enjoy the sweet and spiced indulgence!

Honey Lavender Ice Cream

Ingredients:

- 2 cups heavy cream
- 1 cup whole milk
- 3/4 cup granulated sugar
- 1/4 cup honey
- 2 tablespoons dried lavender buds (culinary-grade)
- 5 large egg yolks
- 1 teaspoon vanilla extract

Instructions:

1. Infuse the Milk and Cream:

    In a saucepan, combine the heavy cream, whole milk, honey, and dried lavender buds. Heat the mixture over medium heat until it just begins to simmer.
    Once it simmers, remove the saucepan from heat and let the lavender steep in the mixture for about 20-30 minutes to infuse the flavors.
    After steeping, strain the mixture to remove the lavender buds. Return the infused milk and cream to the saucepan.

2. Make the Ice Cream Base:

    In a separate bowl, whisk together the egg yolks and granulated sugar until the mixture becomes pale and slightly thickened.
    Slowly pour the infused milk and cream over the egg yolk mixture, whisking constantly to prevent the eggs from curdling.
    Transfer the combined mixture back to the saucepan.
    Heat the mixture over medium heat, stirring constantly, until it thickens and coats the back of a spoon. Do not let it boil.
    Once thickened, remove from heat and stir in the vanilla extract.

3. Chill the Mixture:

    Allow the ice cream base to cool to room temperature.
    Cover the bowl with plastic wrap and refrigerate for at least 4 hours or overnight to ensure it's well-chilled.

4. Freeze:

Pour the chilled Honey Lavender Ice Cream base into an ice cream maker and churn according to the manufacturer's instructions.

5. Serve:

    Transfer the churned ice cream into a lidded container.
    Freeze for an additional few hours or until it reaches your desired consistency.

6. Scoop and Enjoy:

    Scoop the Honey Lavender Ice Cream into bowls or cones.
    Relish in the subtle floral and sweet flavors of homemade Honey Lavender Ice Cream.
    Serve and enjoy this sophisticated and unique frozen treat!

This Honey Lavender Ice Cream offers a delightful combination of floral lavender and sweet honey, creating a truly unique and sophisticated flavor profile. It's a perfect choice for those who appreciate the delicate and aromatic qualities of lavender in their desserts. Enjoy the elegance of this homemade treat!

Mocha Almond Fudge Ice Cream

Ingredients:

For the Mocha Almond Fudge Swirl:

- 1/2 cup strong brewed coffee, cooled
- 1/2 cup chocolate fudge sauce (store-bought or homemade)
- 1/2 cup chopped almonds, toasted

For the Ice Cream Base:

- 2 cups heavy cream
- 1 cup whole milk
- 3/4 cup granulated sugar
- 3 tablespoons unsweetened cocoa powder
- 2 tablespoons instant coffee or espresso powder
- 1 teaspoon vanilla extract
- Pinch of salt

Instructions:

1. Prepare the Mocha Almond Fudge Swirl:

    In a small bowl, mix the strong brewed coffee and chocolate fudge sauce until well combined.
    Toast the chopped almonds in a dry skillet over medium heat until they are lightly browned and fragrant. Set aside to cool.

2. Make the Ice Cream Base:

    In a mixing bowl, whisk together the heavy cream, whole milk, granulated sugar, cocoa powder, instant coffee or espresso powder, vanilla extract, and a pinch of salt until the sugar and coffee dissolve.

3. Add Mocha Almond Fudge Swirl:

    Pour a small amount of the ice cream base into the ice cream maker.
    Drizzle some of the mocha almond fudge swirl over the ice cream base.
    Repeat the process, layering the ice cream base and mocha almond fudge swirl until both are used up.

4. Freeze:

Pour the layered mixture into the ice cream maker and churn according to the manufacturer's instructions.

5. Add Toasted Almonds:

    During the last few minutes of churning, add the toasted chopped almonds to the ice cream maker, allowing them to evenly mix into the ice cream.

6. Serve:

    Transfer the churned Mocha Almond Fudge Ice Cream into a lidded container.
    Freeze for an additional few hours or until it reaches your desired consistency.

7. Scoop and Enjoy:

    Scoop the Mocha Almond Fudge Ice Cream into bowls or cones.
    Delight in the rich and decadent flavors of homemade Mocha Almond Fudge Ice Cream.
    Serve and enjoy this irresistible frozen treat!

This Mocha Almond Fudge Ice Cream combines the bold flavors of coffee and chocolate with the crunch of toasted almonds, creating a luscious and indulgent dessert experience. It's perfect for coffee and chocolate lovers alike. Enjoy the creamy goodness!

Blueberry Cheesecake Ice Cream

Ingredients:

For the Blueberry Swirl:

- 1 cup fresh or frozen blueberries
- 1/4 cup granulated sugar
- 1 tablespoon lemon juice

For the Cheesecake Base:

- 2 cups cream cheese, softened
- 1 cup heavy cream
- 1 cup whole milk
- 3/4 cup granulated sugar
- 1 teaspoon vanilla extract
- 1/2 cup graham cracker crumbs

Instructions:

1. Prepare the Blueberry Swirl:

In a saucepan, combine the blueberries, granulated sugar, and lemon juice.
Cook over medium heat until the blueberries burst and the mixture thickens into a syrup.
Set aside to cool.

2. Make the Cheesecake Base:

In a mixing bowl, beat the cream cheese until smooth and creamy.
Add the heavy cream, whole milk, granulated sugar, and vanilla extract to the cream cheese. Mix until well combined.
Stir in the graham cracker crumbs to add the cheesecake crust flavor.

3. Add Blueberry Swirl:

Pour a small amount of the cheesecake base into the ice cream maker.
Spoon some of the blueberry swirl over the cheesecake base.
Repeat the process, layering the cheesecake base and blueberry swirl until both are used up.

4. Freeze:

Pour the layered mixture into the ice cream maker and churn according to the manufacturer's instructions.

5. Serve:

Transfer the churned Blueberry Cheesecake Ice Cream into a lidded container.
Freeze for an additional few hours or until it reaches your desired consistency.

6. Scoop and Enjoy:

Scoop the Blueberry Cheesecake Ice Cream into bowls or cones.
Relish in the creamy and fruity flavors of homemade Blueberry Cheesecake Ice Cream.
Serve and enjoy this decadent frozen treat that captures the essence of blueberry cheesecake!

This Blueberry Cheesecake Ice Cream offers a luxurious blend of velvety cheesecake and sweet blueberry swirls, creating a delightful frozen dessert. It's a perfect way to enjoy the classic flavors of blueberry cheesecake in a cool and creamy form. Indulge in the sweetness!

Tiramisu Ice Cream

Ingredients:

For the Tiramisu Swirl:

- 1/2 cup strong brewed coffee, cooled
- 2 tablespoons coffee liqueur (e.g., Kahlúa)
- 1/4 cup cocoa powder
- 1/4 cup mascarpone cheese
- 1/4 cup sweetened condensed milk

For the Ice Cream Base:

- 2 cups heavy cream
- 1 cup whole milk
- 3/4 cup granulated sugar
- 3 large egg yolks
- 1 teaspoon vanilla extract

Optional:

- Ladyfinger cookies, chopped

Instructions:

1. Prepare the Tiramisu Swirl:

    In a bowl, combine the strong brewed coffee, coffee liqueur, and cocoa powder. Mix until the cocoa powder is fully dissolved.
    In a separate bowl, whisk together the mascarpone cheese and sweetened condensed milk until smooth.
    Gradually add the coffee mixture to the mascarpone mixture, whisking continuously to ensure a smooth and creamy consistency. Set aside.

2. Make the Ice Cream Base:

    In a saucepan, heat the heavy cream, whole milk, and granulated sugar over medium heat until it just begins to simmer. Do not let it boil.
    In a separate bowl, whisk the egg yolks. Slowly pour a small amount of the hot cream mixture into the egg yolks, whisking continuously to temper the eggs.

Pour the tempered egg mixture back into the saucepan with the remaining hot cream mixture. Cook over medium heat, stirring constantly, until the mixture thickens and coats the back of a spoon. Do not let it boil.
Remove the saucepan from heat and stir in the vanilla extract.

3. Add Tiramisu Swirl:

    Allow the ice cream base to cool to room temperature.
    Pour a small amount of the ice cream base into the ice cream maker.
    Drizzle some of the tiramisu swirl over the ice cream base.
    Repeat the process, layering the ice cream base and tiramisu swirl until both are used up.

4. Freeze:

    Pour the layered mixture into the ice cream maker and churn according to the manufacturer's instructions.

5. Optional:

    During the last few minutes of churning, add chopped ladyfinger cookies to the ice cream maker, allowing them to mix in.

6. Serve:

    Transfer the churned Tiramisu Ice Cream into a lidded container.
    Freeze for an additional few hours or until it reaches your desired consistency.

7. Scoop and Enjoy:

    Scoop the Tiramisu Ice Cream into bowls or cones.
    Delight in the rich and sophisticated flavors of homemade Tiramisu Ice Cream.
    Serve and enjoy this frozen treat inspired by the classic Italian dessert!

This Tiramisu Ice Cream captures the essence of the beloved coffee-flavored dessert in a cool and creamy form. The addition of a tiramisu swirl and optional ladyfinger cookies provides layers of flavor reminiscent of the classic dessert. Enjoy the luxurious taste of tiramisu in every scoop!

White Chocolate Raspberry Ripple Ice Cream

Ingredients:

For the Raspberry Ripple:

- 1 cup fresh or frozen raspberries
- 1/4 cup granulated sugar
- 1 tablespoon lemon juice

For the White Chocolate Base:

- 2 cups heavy cream
- 1 cup whole milk
- 3/4 cup granulated sugar
- 8 ounces white chocolate, chopped
- 1 teaspoon vanilla extract
- A pinch of salt

Instructions:

1. Prepare the Raspberry Ripple:

    In a saucepan, combine the raspberries, granulated sugar, and lemon juice.
    Cook over medium heat until the raspberries break down and the mixture thickens into a syrup. Set aside to cool.

2. Make the White Chocolate Base:

    In a separate saucepan, heat the heavy cream, whole milk, and granulated sugar over medium heat until it just begins to simmer. Do not let it boil.
    Place the chopped white chocolate in a heatproof bowl.
    Pour the hot cream mixture over the white chocolate. Let it sit for a minute, then stir until the white chocolate is fully melted and incorporated.
    Stir in the vanilla extract and a pinch of salt.

3. Add Raspberry Ripple:

    Allow the white chocolate base to cool to room temperature.
    Pour a small amount of the white chocolate base into the ice cream maker.
    Spoon some of the raspberry ripple over the white chocolate base.
    Repeat the process, layering the white chocolate base and raspberry ripple until both are used up.

4. Freeze:

> Pour the layered mixture into the ice cream maker and churn according to the manufacturer's instructions.

5. Serve:

> Transfer the churned White Chocolate Raspberry Ripple Ice Cream into a lidded container.
> Freeze for an additional few hours or until it reaches your desired consistency.

6. Scoop and Enjoy:

> Scoop the White Chocolate Raspberry Ripple Ice Cream into bowls or cones.
> Relish in the creamy white chocolate base swirled with sweet and tangy raspberry ripple.
> Serve and enjoy this decadent frozen treat with the perfect balance of flavors!

This White Chocolate Raspberry Ripple Ice Cream combines the richness of white chocolate with the vibrant sweetness of raspberry ripple, creating a luxurious and delightful dessert. It's a perfect choice for those who appreciate the harmonious pairing of fruity and chocolatey goodness. Indulge in every spoonful!

Key Lime Pie Ice Cream

Ingredients:

For the Key Lime Pie Swirl:

- 1/2 cup key lime juice (freshly squeezed)
- 1 tablespoon key lime zest
- 1/2 cup sweetened condensed milk
- 1/4 cup graham cracker crumbs

For the Ice Cream Base:

- 2 cups heavy cream
- 1 cup whole milk
- 3/4 cup granulated sugar
- 1 teaspoon vanilla extract
- A pinch of salt

Instructions:

1. Prepare the Key Lime Pie Swirl:

    In a bowl, combine the key lime juice, key lime zest, sweetened condensed milk, and graham cracker crumbs. Mix until well combined. Set aside.

2. Make the Ice Cream Base:

    In a mixing bowl, whisk together the heavy cream, whole milk, granulated sugar, vanilla extract, and a pinch of salt until the sugar is dissolved.

3. Add Key Lime Pie Swirl:

    Pour a small amount of the ice cream base into the ice cream maker.
    Spoon some of the key lime pie swirl mixture over the ice cream base.
    Repeat the process, layering the ice cream base and key lime pie swirl until both are used up.

4. Freeze:

    Pour the layered mixture into the ice cream maker and churn according to the manufacturer's instructions.

5. Serve:

Transfer the churned Key Lime Pie Ice Cream into a lidded container.
Freeze for an additional few hours or until it reaches your desired consistency.

6. Scoop and Enjoy:

Scoop the Key Lime Pie Ice Cream into bowls or cones.
Revel in the zesty and creamy goodness of homemade Key Lime Pie Ice Cream.
Serve and enjoy this tropical and citrusy frozen treat inspired by the classic Key Lime Pie!

This Key Lime Pie Ice Cream captures the essence of the iconic dessert with its tangy key lime swirl and the creamy richness of the ice cream base. The addition of graham cracker crumbs adds a delightful pie crust crunch. It's a perfect choice for a refreshing and tropical frozen dessert. Enjoy the tropical vibes in every spoonful!

Pomegranate Sorbet

Ingredients:

- 2 cups pomegranate juice (freshly squeezed or store-bought)
- 1/2 cup granulated sugar
- 1/4 cup water
- 1 tablespoon freshly squeezed lemon juice (optional, for added brightness)

Instructions:

1. Prepare the Simple Syrup:

    In a small saucepan, combine the granulated sugar and water.
    Heat over medium heat, stirring occasionally, until the sugar completely dissolves. This will create a simple syrup.
    Remove the saucepan from heat and let the simple syrup cool to room temperature.

2. Mix Pomegranate Juice:

    In a mixing bowl, combine the pomegranate juice and the cooled simple syrup.
    If desired, add freshly squeezed lemon juice for an extra burst of citrus flavor.

3. Chill the Mixture:

    Place the mixture in the refrigerator and let it chill for at least 2 hours or until it's thoroughly chilled.

4. Freeze in Ice Cream Maker:

    Pour the chilled pomegranate mixture into your ice cream maker.
    Churn the mixture according to the manufacturer's instructions until it reaches a slushy, sorbet-like consistency.

5. Transfer to Container:

    Transfer the churned sorbet into a lidded container.

6. Final Freeze:

    Freeze the sorbet for an additional 2-4 hours or until it firms up to your preferred texture.

7. Scoop and Enjoy:

    Scoop the Pomegranate Sorbet into bowls or cones.

Enjoy the refreshing and tangy taste of homemade Pomegranate Sorbet.

This Pomegranate Sorbet is a delightful and palate-cleansing dessert that captures the essence of fresh pomegranate juice. It's perfect for a light and fruity treat on a warm day. Enjoy the burst of flavor and the cool, refreshing sensation with every spoonful!

Avocado Lime Ice Cream

Ingredients:

- 2 ripe avocados, peeled and pitted
- 1 cup sweetened condensed milk
- 1 cup whole milk or coconut milk (for a dairy-free option)
- 1/4 cup fresh lime juice (approximately 2-3 limes)
- Zest of 1 lime
- 1 teaspoon vanilla extract
- A pinch of salt

Instructions:

1. Prepare the Avocado Base:

    In a blender or food processor, combine the ripe avocados, sweetened condensed milk, whole milk or coconut milk, lime juice, lime zest, vanilla extract, and a pinch of salt.
    Blend until the mixture is smooth and well combined.

2. Chill the Mixture:

    Pour the avocado and lime mixture into a bowl and refrigerate for at least 2 hours or until thoroughly chilled.

3. Freeze in Ice Cream Maker:

    Once chilled, pour the avocado and lime mixture into your ice cream maker. Churn the mixture according to the manufacturer's instructions until it reaches a creamy ice cream consistency.

4. Transfer to Container:

    Transfer the churned ice cream into a lidded container.

5. Final Freeze:

    Freeze the ice cream for an additional 2-4 hours or until it firms up to your preferred texture.

6. Scoop and Enjoy:

Scoop the Avocado Lime Ice Cream into bowls or cones.
Relish in the unique and creamy combination of avocado and lime.
Serve and enjoy this tropical and citrusy frozen treat!

This Avocado Lime Ice Cream offers a delightful and unexpected flavor combination. The creamy texture of ripe avocados blends seamlessly with the zesty kick of fresh lime, creating a refreshing dessert with a tropical twist. Indulge in the creamy goodness with every spoonful!

Dark Chocolate Orange Ice Cream

Ingredients:

- 2 cups heavy cream
- 1 cup whole milk
- 3/4 cup granulated sugar
- 8 ounces dark chocolate, finely chopped
- Zest of 2 oranges
- 1/4 cup fresh orange juice
- 1 teaspoon vanilla extract
- A pinch of salt

Instructions:

1. Melt Dark Chocolate:

    Place the finely chopped dark chocolate in a heatproof bowl.
    In a saucepan, heat the heavy cream, whole milk, and granulated sugar over medium heat until it just begins to simmer. Do not let it boil.
    Pour the hot cream mixture over the dark chocolate. Let it sit for a minute, then stir until the chocolate is fully melted and incorporated.

2. Add Orange Zest and Juice:

    Stir in the orange zest and fresh orange juice into the melted chocolate mixture.
    Add vanilla extract and a pinch of salt. Mix until well combined.

3. Chill the Mixture:

    Allow the chocolate and orange mixture to cool to room temperature.
    Once cooled, refrigerate the mixture for at least 2 hours or until thoroughly chilled.

4. Freeze in Ice Cream Maker:

    Pour the chilled chocolate and orange mixture into your ice cream maker.
    Churn the mixture according to the manufacturer's instructions until it reaches a creamy ice cream consistency.

5. Transfer to Container:

    Transfer the churned ice cream into a lidded container.

6. Final Freeze:

> Freeze the ice cream for an additional 2-4 hours or until it firms up to your preferred texture.

7. Scoop and Enjoy:

> Scoop the Dark Chocolate Orange Ice Cream into bowls or cones.
> Delight in the luxurious combination of dark chocolate and bright orange flavors.
> Serve and enjoy this sophisticated and indulgent frozen treat!

This Dark Chocolate Orange Ice Cream brings together the velvety richness of dark chocolate with the vibrant and citrusy notes of orange. The result is a decadent and refreshing dessert that's perfect for satisfying your chocolate cravings with a citrusy twist. Enjoy the harmonious blend of flavors in every spoonful!

Caramelized Banana Ice Cream

Ingredients:

- 4 ripe bananas, peeled and sliced
- 1/2 cup brown sugar
- 1/4 cup unsalted butter
- 2 cups heavy cream
- 1 cup whole milk
- 3/4 cup granulated sugar
- 1 teaspoon vanilla extract
- A pinch of salt

Instructions:

1. Caramelize the Bananas:

> In a skillet, melt the unsalted butter over medium heat.
> Sprinkle brown sugar evenly over the melted butter.
> Add the sliced bananas to the skillet and cook for 3-5 minutes, stirring occasionally, until the bananas are caramelized and coated in the brown sugar-butter mixture.
> Remove the skillet from heat and let the caramelized bananas cool.

2. Prepare the Ice Cream Base:

> In a blender or food processor, combine the caramelized bananas and any residual caramelized sauce.
> Blend until you have a smooth banana puree.
> In a mixing bowl, whisk together the heavy cream, whole milk, granulated sugar, vanilla extract, and a pinch of salt.
> Add the banana puree to the cream mixture and whisk until well combined.

3. Chill the Mixture:

> Place the banana and cream mixture in the refrigerator and let it chill for at least 2 hours or until thoroughly chilled.

4. Freeze in Ice Cream Maker:

> Once chilled, pour the banana and cream mixture into your ice cream maker.

Churn the mixture according to the manufacturer's instructions until it reaches a creamy ice cream consistency.

5. Transfer to Container:

    Transfer the churned ice cream into a lidded container.

6. Final Freeze:

    Freeze the ice cream for an additional 2-4 hours or until it firms up to your preferred texture.

7. Scoop and Enjoy:

    Scoop the Caramelized Banana Ice Cream into bowls or cones.
    Relish in the sweet and caramel-infused banana flavor.
    Serve and enjoy this delightful frozen treat!

This Caramelized Banana Ice Cream is a rich and creamy dessert with the added depth of flavor from caramelized bananas. It's a perfect way to elevate the classic banana ice cream with a touch of indulgent caramelization. Enjoy the luscious banana goodness in every spoonful!

Nutella Swirl Ice Cream

Ingredients:

- 2 cups heavy cream
- 1 cup whole milk
- 3/4 cup granulated sugar
- 1/2 cup Nutella (chocolate hazelnut spread)
- 1 teaspoon vanilla extract
- A pinch of salt

Instructions:

1. Prepare the Ice Cream Base:

    In a mixing bowl, whisk together the heavy cream, whole milk, granulated sugar, vanilla extract, and a pinch of salt until the sugar is dissolved.
    Warm the mixture over medium heat, stirring continuously, until it just begins to simmer. Do not let it boil.
    Remove the mixture from heat and let it cool to room temperature.

2. Add Nutella Swirl:

    Once the ice cream base is cooled, heat the Nutella in a microwave-safe bowl for about 20-30 seconds to soften it.
    Gently fold in the Nutella into the ice cream base, creating swirls but not fully incorporating it. You want the Nutella to create a marbled effect.

3. Chill the Mixture:

    Place the Nutella-swirled ice cream base in the refrigerator and let it chill for at least 2 hours or until thoroughly chilled.

4. Freeze in Ice Cream Maker:

    Pour the chilled Nutella-swirled mixture into your ice cream maker.
    Churn the mixture according to the manufacturer's instructions until it reaches a creamy ice cream consistency.

5. Transfer to Container:

    Transfer the churned ice cream into a lidded container.

6. Final Freeze:

Freeze the ice cream for an additional 2-4 hours or until it firms up to your preferred texture.

7. Scoop and Enjoy:

Scoop the Nutella Swirl Ice Cream into bowls or cones.
Savor the rich and decadent swirls of Nutella in every bite.
Serve and relish this heavenly chocolate hazelnut frozen delight!

This Nutella Swirl Ice Cream combines the creamy goodness of homemade ice cream with the irresistible flavor of Nutella. The result is a luscious and indulgent treat that chocolate and hazelnut enthusiasts will adore. Enjoy the delightful Nutella swirls in every scoop!

Balsamic Strawberry Ice Cream

Ingredients:

- 2 cups fresh strawberries, hulled and sliced
- 1/2 cup balsamic vinegar
- 1 cup granulated sugar
- 2 cups heavy cream
- 1 cup whole milk
- 1 teaspoon vanilla extract
- A pinch of salt

Instructions:

1. Balsamic Strawberry Compote:

    In a saucepan, combine the sliced strawberries, balsamic vinegar, and half of the granulated sugar.
    Heat over medium heat, stirring occasionally, until the strawberries break down and the mixture thickens into a compote. This should take about 10-15 minutes.
    Remove from heat and let the strawberry balsamic compote cool to room temperature.

2. Prepare the Ice Cream Base:

    In a mixing bowl, whisk together the heavy cream, whole milk, the remaining sugar, vanilla extract, and a pinch of salt until the sugar is dissolved.
    Add the cooled balsamic strawberry compote to the ice cream base and gently fold it in, creating swirls but not fully incorporating it.

3. Chill the Mixture:

    Place the balsamic strawberry ice cream base in the refrigerator and let it chill for at least 2 hours or until thoroughly chilled.

4. Freeze in Ice Cream Maker:

    Pour the chilled balsamic strawberry mixture into your ice cream maker.
    Churn the mixture according to the manufacturer's instructions until it reaches a creamy ice cream consistency.

5. Transfer to Container:

    Transfer the churned ice cream into a lidded container.

6. Final Freeze:

> Freeze the ice cream for an additional 2-4 hours or until it firms up to your preferred texture.

7. Scoop and Enjoy:

> Scoop the Balsamic Strawberry Ice Cream into bowls or cones.
> Relish the sweet and tangy swirls of balsamic-infused strawberries in each bite.
> Serve and enjoy this unique and refreshing frozen treat!

This Balsamic Strawberry Ice Cream offers a sophisticated twist to traditional strawberry ice cream. The addition of balsamic vinegar enhances the natural sweetness of strawberries, creating a balanced and delightful flavor. Enjoy the refreshing taste of summer with this delicious homemade treat!

Red Velvet Ice Cream

Ingredients:

- 2 cups heavy cream
- 1 cup whole milk
- 3/4 cup granulated sugar
- 3 tablespoons unsweetened cocoa powder
- 2 teaspoons red food coloring
- 1 teaspoon vanilla extract
- 1/2 cup cream cheese, softened
- A pinch of salt
- Red velvet cake crumbs or red velvet cookie pieces (optional, for mix-ins)

Instructions:

1. Prepare the Ice Cream Base:

   In a mixing bowl, whisk together the heavy cream, whole milk, granulated sugar, unsweetened cocoa powder, red food coloring, vanilla extract, and a pinch of salt until the sugar is dissolved.
   In a separate bowl, whisk the softened cream cheese until smooth.
   Add a small amount of the cream mixture to the cream cheese and whisk until well combined. Gradually add more of the cream mixture, whisking continuously to avoid lumps.
   Once the cream cheese mixture is smooth, combine it with the rest of the cream mixture and mix well.

2. Chill the Mixture:

   Place the red velvet ice cream base in the refrigerator and let it chill for at least 2 hours or until thoroughly chilled.

3. Freeze in Ice Cream Maker:

   Pour the chilled red velvet mixture into your ice cream maker.
   Churn the mixture according to the manufacturer's instructions until it reaches a creamy ice cream consistency.

4. Add Mix-Ins (Optional):

During the last few minutes of churning, add red velvet cake crumbs or red velvet cookie pieces for an extra layer of flavor and texture. This step is optional but adds a delightful touch.

5. Transfer to Container:

    Transfer the churned red velvet ice cream into a lidded container.

6. Final Freeze:

    Freeze the ice cream for an additional 2-4 hours or until it firms up to your preferred texture.

7. Scoop and Enjoy:

    Scoop the Red Velvet Ice Cream into bowls or cones.
    Delight in the rich, vibrant, and velvety flavor of this homemade frozen treat.
    Serve and enjoy this decadent dessert inspired by the classic red velvet cake!

This Red Velvet Ice Cream captures the essence of the beloved red velvet cake in a cool and creamy form. The addition of red food coloring and cocoa powder creates the iconic red color and chocolatey flavor. Indulge in the luxurious taste of red velvet in every spoonful!

Brown Butter Pecan Ice Cream

Ingredients:

- 2 cups pecan halves
- 1 cup unsalted butter
- 2 cups heavy cream
- 1 cup whole milk
- 3/4 cup brown sugar, packed
- 1/2 cup granulated sugar
- 1 teaspoon vanilla extract
- A pinch of salt

Instructions:

1. Toast the Pecans:

    Preheat your oven to 350°F (175°C).
    Spread the pecan halves on a baking sheet in a single layer.
    Toast the pecans in the preheated oven for about 8-10 minutes, or until they become fragrant. Make sure to watch them closely to avoid burning. Once toasted, remove from the oven and let them cool.
    Chop the toasted pecans into smaller pieces. Set aside.

2. Brown the Butter:

    In a saucepan over medium heat, melt the unsalted butter.
    Continue to cook the butter, stirring frequently, until it starts to brown and develop a nutty aroma. Be attentive to prevent burning.
    Once browned, remove the saucepan from heat and let the brown butter cool slightly.

3. Prepare the Ice Cream Base:

    In a mixing bowl, whisk together the heavy cream, whole milk, brown sugar, granulated sugar, vanilla extract, and a pinch of salt until the sugars are dissolved.
    Slowly pour the slightly cooled brown butter into the cream mixture while whisking continuously. Ensure that the brown butter is well incorporated.

4. Chill the Mixture:

Place the brown butter pecan ice cream base in the refrigerator and let it chill for at least 2 hours or until thoroughly chilled.

5. Freeze in Ice Cream Maker:

   Pour the chilled brown butter pecan mixture into your ice cream maker.
   Churn the mixture according to the manufacturer's instructions until it reaches a creamy ice cream consistency.

6. Add Toasted Pecans:

   During the last few minutes of churning, add the chopped toasted pecans to the ice cream, allowing them to mix evenly.

7. Transfer to Container:

   Transfer the churned brown butter pecan ice cream into a lidded container.

8. Final Freeze:

   Freeze the ice cream for an additional 2-4 hours or until it firms up to your preferred texture.

9. Scoop and Enjoy:

   Scoop the Brown Butter Pecan Ice Cream into bowls or cones.
   Revel in the rich, nutty, and buttery flavor of this homemade frozen delight.
   Serve and savor the decadence of brown butter and pecans in every spoonful!

This Brown Butter Pecan Ice Cream offers a sophisticated twist on the classic pecan ice cream by incorporating the rich and nutty flavor of browned butter. The result is a velvety and indulgent frozen treat with a delightful crunch from the toasted pecans. Enjoy the luxurious taste of brown butter and pecans in this homemade ice cream!

Cardamom Rose Ice Cream

Ingredients:

- 2 cups heavy cream
- 1 cup whole milk
- 3/4 cup granulated sugar
- 1 teaspoon ground cardamom
- 1 teaspoon rose water
- 1 teaspoon vanilla extract
- A pinch of salt
- Dried rose petals for garnish (optional)

Instructions:

1. Prepare the Ice Cream Base:

    In a mixing bowl, whisk together the heavy cream, whole milk, granulated sugar, ground cardamom, rose water, vanilla extract, and a pinch of salt until the sugar is dissolved.

2. Chill the Mixture:

    Place the cardamom rose ice cream base in the refrigerator and let it chill for at least 2 hours or until thoroughly chilled.

3. Freeze in Ice Cream Maker:

    Pour the chilled cardamom rose mixture into your ice cream maker.
    Churn the mixture according to the manufacturer's instructions until it reaches a creamy ice cream consistency.

4. Transfer to Container:

    Transfer the churned cardamom rose ice cream into a lidded container.

5. Final Freeze:

    Freeze the ice cream for an additional 2-4 hours or until it firms up to your preferred texture.

6. Scoop and Garnish:

    Scoop the Cardamom Rose Ice Cream into bowls or cones.
    Optionally, garnish with dried rose petals for a touch of elegance.

7. Serve and Enjoy:

> Delight in the aromatic blend of cardamom and rose in every spoonful.
> Serve and enjoy this unique and fragrant frozen dessert!

This Cardamom Rose Ice Cream offers a captivating fusion of warm cardamom spice and the delicate floral essence of rose water. The result is a luxurious and aromatic ice cream that transports you to a world of exotic flavors. Experience the enchanting taste of cardamom and rose in this homemade frozen treat!

Earl Grey Tea Ice Cream

Ingredients:

- 2 cups heavy cream
- 1 cup whole milk
- 3/4 cup granulated sugar
- 4-5 Earl Grey tea bags or loose tea leaves
- 1 teaspoon vanilla extract
- A pinch of salt

Instructions:

1. Infuse the Milk and Cream with Earl Grey Tea:

    In a saucepan, combine the heavy cream and whole milk over medium heat. Heat the mixture until it just begins to simmer, then remove it from the heat. Add the Earl Grey tea bags or loose tea leaves to the hot cream mixture. Let it steep for about 15-20 minutes, allowing the tea to infuse its flavor into the liquid. Strain the tea leaves or remove the tea bags, pressing them gently to extract any remaining flavor.

2. Prepare the Ice Cream Base:

    In a mixing bowl, whisk together the infused cream and milk, granulated sugar, vanilla extract, and a pinch of salt until the sugar is dissolved.

3. Chill the Mixture:

    Place the Earl Grey tea ice cream base in the refrigerator and let it chill for at least 2 hours or until thoroughly chilled.

4. Freeze in Ice Cream Maker:

    Pour the chilled Earl Grey tea mixture into your ice cream maker.
    Churn the mixture according to the manufacturer's instructions until it reaches a creamy ice cream consistency.

5. Transfer to Container:

    Transfer the churned Earl Grey tea ice cream into a lidded container.

6. Final Freeze:

> Freeze the ice cream for an additional 2-4 hours or until it firms up to your preferred texture.

7. Scoop and Enjoy:

> Scoop the Earl Grey Tea Ice Cream into bowls or cones.
> Savor the elegant and aromatic notes of Earl Grey tea in each spoonful.
> Serve and enjoy this refined and sophisticated frozen dessert!

This Earl Grey Tea Ice Cream captures the essence of the classic tea blend, offering a subtle and aromatic experience with each bite. The creamy texture combined with the distinctive flavor of Earl Grey makes for a delightful frozen treat. Indulge in the refined taste of tea in this homemade ice cream creation!

S'mores Ice Cream

Ingredients:

- 2 cups heavy cream
- 1 cup whole milk
- 3/4 cup granulated sugar
- 1 teaspoon vanilla extract
- 1 cup chocolate chunks or chocolate chips
- 1 cup mini marshmallows
- 1 cup graham cracker pieces (crushed)
- Additional chocolate, marshmallows, and graham crackers for mix-ins (optional)

Instructions:

1. Prepare the Ice Cream Base:

    In a mixing bowl, whisk together the heavy cream, whole milk, granulated sugar, and vanilla extract until the sugar is dissolved.

2. Freeze in Ice Cream Maker:

    Pour the ice cream base into your ice cream maker.
    Churn the mixture according to the manufacturer's instructions until it reaches a creamy ice cream consistency.

3. Add Mix-Ins:

    During the last few minutes of churning, add chocolate chunks or chips, mini marshmallows, and graham cracker pieces. This step adds extra texture and flavor to your S'mores Ice Cream.
    Optionally, fold in additional chocolate chunks, marshmallows, and graham cracker pieces for larger mix-ins.

4. Transfer to Container:

    Transfer the churned S'mores Ice Cream into a lidded container.

5. Final Freeze:

    Freeze the ice cream for an additional 2-4 hours or until it firms up to your preferred texture.

6. Scoop and Enjoy:

Scoop the S'mores Ice Cream into bowls or cones.
Relish the classic campfire flavors of chocolate, marshmallow, and graham crackers in each delicious spoonful.
Serve and enjoy this homemade frozen treat that captures the essence of everyone's favorite fireside dessert!

This S'mores Ice Cream brings the beloved campfire treat to a new level of cool and creamy goodness. The combination of chocolate, marshmallows, and graham crackers creates a nostalgic and irresistible flavor profile. Indulge in the essence of S'mores with this delightful homemade ice cream!

Chocolate Hazelnut Gelato

Ingredients:

- 2 cups whole milk
- 1 cup heavy cream
- 3/4 cup granulated sugar
- 1/2 cup unsweetened cocoa powder
- 1/2 cup Nutella or chocolate hazelnut spread
- 1 teaspoon vanilla extract
- 1/2 cup chopped hazelnuts, toasted (for garnish, optional)

Instructions:

1. Prepare the Gelato Base:

    In a saucepan, whisk together the whole milk, heavy cream, granulated sugar, and unsweetened cocoa powder over medium heat.
    Heat the mixture until it just begins to simmer, stirring constantly to dissolve the sugar and cocoa.
    Once simmering, remove the saucepan from heat.

2. Add Nutella and Vanilla:

    Add Nutella or chocolate hazelnut spread to the hot milk and cream mixture.
    Whisk until the Nutella is fully incorporated.
    Stir in the vanilla extract, ensuring a smooth and uniform consistency.

3. Chill the Mixture:

    Transfer the gelato base to a bowl and let it cool to room temperature.
    Cover the bowl and refrigerate the mixture for at least 4 hours or overnight to ensure it is thoroughly chilled.

4. Freeze in Gelato Maker or Ice Cream Maker:

    Pour the chilled chocolate hazelnut gelato base into your gelato maker or ice cream maker.
    Churn the mixture according to the manufacturer's instructions until it reaches a creamy gelato consistency.

5. Garnish and Freeze:

If desired, fold in chopped hazelnuts during the last few minutes of churning or sprinkle them over the gelato after transferring it to a container.

Transfer the churned gelato into a lidded container.

Freeze the gelato for an additional 2-4 hours or until it firms up to your preferred texture.

6. Scoop and Enjoy:

Scoop the Chocolate Hazelnut Gelato into bowls or cones.

Delight in the velvety texture and rich flavor of this decadent homemade frozen treat.

Serve and savor the irresistible combination of chocolate and hazelnut in every spoonful!

This Chocolate Hazelnut Gelato captures the essence of the classic Italian treat, offering a luxurious blend of creamy chocolate and the nutty goodness of hazelnuts. Indulge in the rich and velvety texture of this homemade gelato for a delightful frozen dessert experience!

Guava Passionfruit Sorbet

Ingredients:

- 3 cups guava juice (freshly squeezed or store-bought)
- 1 cup passionfruit puree (fresh or frozen)
- 1 cup simple syrup (equal parts water and sugar, dissolved)
- 1 tablespoon lime juice (optional, for a citrusy kick)
- Zest of one lime (optional, for added citrus aroma)

Instructions:

1. Prepare Simple Syrup:

    In a small saucepan, combine equal parts water and sugar.
    Heat the mixture over medium heat, stirring until the sugar completely dissolves.
    Allow the simple syrup to cool, and then refrigerate until it's chilled.

2. Mix Sorbet Base:

    In a large bowl, combine guava juice, passionfruit puree, and chilled simple syrup.
    Optionally, add lime juice for a citrusy kick and zest of one lime for added aroma.
    Mix the ingredients thoroughly to ensure a well-combined sorbet base.

3. Chill the Mixture:

    Place the sorbet mixture in the refrigerator and let it chill for at least 2-4 hours or until thoroughly chilled.

4. Freeze in Sorbet Maker:

    Pour the chilled guava passionfruit sorbet mixture into your sorbet maker.
    Churn the mixture according to the manufacturer's instructions until it reaches a smooth and frozen sorbet consistency.

5. Transfer to Container:

    Transfer the churned sorbet into a lidded container.

6. Final Freeze:

    Freeze the sorbet for an additional 2-4 hours or until it firms up to your preferred texture.

7. Scoop and Enjoy:

Scoop the Guava Passionfruit Sorbet into bowls or cones.
Relish the tropical and refreshing flavors of this homemade sorbet.
Serve and enjoy the cool and fruity experience of guava and passionfruit!

This Guava Passionfruit Sorbet is a delightful way to enjoy the tropical essence of guava and passionfruit in a cool and refreshing frozen treat. Indulge in the bright and exotic flavors of this homemade sorbet for a burst of tropical delight!

White Chocolate Macadamia Nut Ice Cream

Ingredients:

- 2 cups heavy cream
- 1 cup whole milk
- 3/4 cup granulated sugar
- 1 cup white chocolate chips
- 1 teaspoon vanilla extract
- 1 cup macadamia nuts, chopped and toasted

Instructions:

1. Prepare the Ice Cream Base:

    In a saucepan, combine the heavy cream, whole milk, and granulated sugar over medium heat.
    Stir the mixture until it begins to simmer, ensuring the sugar is completely dissolved.
    Once simmering, remove the saucepan from heat.

2. Add White Chocolate:

    Add the white chocolate chips to the hot cream mixture. Stir until the white chocolate is fully melted and incorporated.

3. Cool the Mixture:

    Allow the white chocolate cream mixture to cool to room temperature.
    Cover the bowl and refrigerate for at least 4 hours or overnight to ensure it is thoroughly chilled.

4. Toast Macadamia Nuts:

    In a dry pan, toast the chopped macadamia nuts over medium heat until they are lightly browned and fragrant. Be sure to stir frequently to avoid burning.
    Allow the toasted macadamia nuts to cool completely.

5. Freeze in Ice Cream Maker:

    Pour the chilled white chocolate cream mixture into your ice cream maker.

Churn the mixture according to the manufacturer's instructions until it reaches a creamy ice cream consistency.

6. Add Macadamia Nuts:

    During the last few minutes of churning, add the toasted and cooled macadamia nuts. This step ensures that the nuts are evenly distributed throughout the ice cream.

7. Transfer to Container:

    Transfer the churned White Chocolate Macadamia Nut Ice Cream into a lidded container.

8. Final Freeze:

    Freeze the ice cream for an additional 2-4 hours or until it firms up to your preferred texture.

9. Scoop and Enjoy:

    Scoop the White Chocolate Macadamia Nut Ice Cream into bowls or cones. Savor the rich and creamy goodness with the delightful combination of white chocolate and toasted macadamia nuts.
    Serve and relish this indulgent homemade frozen treat!

This White Chocolate Macadamia Nut Ice Cream is a heavenly blend of creamy white chocolate and crunchy toasted macadamia nuts. Treat yourself to the luxurious flavors of this homemade ice cream for a delightful and satisfying dessert experience!

Raspberry Lemonade Sorbet

Ingredients:

- 2 cups fresh or frozen raspberries
- 1 cup freshly squeezed lemon juice (about 6-8 lemons)
- 1 cup granulated sugar
- 1 cup water
- Zest of 1 lemon (optional, for added citrus aroma)

Instructions:

1. Prepare Simple Syrup:

    In a saucepan, combine water and granulated sugar.
    Heat the mixture over medium heat, stirring until the sugar completely dissolves.
    Allow the simple syrup to cool, and then refrigerate until it's chilled.

2. Blend Raspberries:

    In a blender or food processor, puree the raspberries until smooth.
    Strain the raspberry puree through a fine-mesh sieve to remove seeds. You can skip this step if you don't mind the seeds.

3. Mix Sorbet Base:

    In a large bowl, combine the raspberry puree, freshly squeezed lemon juice, chilled simple syrup, and optional lemon zest. Mix well.

4. Chill the Mixture:

    Place the sorbet mixture in the refrigerator and let it chill for at least 2-4 hours or until thoroughly chilled.

5. Freeze in Sorbet Maker:

    Pour the chilled Raspberry Lemonade Sorbet mixture into your sorbet maker. Churn the mixture according to the manufacturer's instructions until it reaches a smooth and frozen sorbet consistency.

6. Transfer to Container:

    Transfer the churned sorbet into a lidded container.

7. Final Freeze:

> Freeze the sorbet for an additional 2-4 hours or until it firms up to your preferred texture.

8. Scoop and Enjoy:

> Scoop the Raspberry Lemonade Sorbet into bowls or cones.
> Relish the bright and tangy flavors of this homemade sorbet.
> Serve and enjoy this cool and refreshing frozen dessert!

This Raspberry Lemonade Sorbet is a delightful and tangy treat, perfect for hot days or anytime you crave a refreshing frozen dessert. Indulge in the natural sweetness of raspberries and the zesty kick of lemon with every spoonful!

Chocolate Chili Ice Cream

Ingredients:

- 2 cups heavy cream
- 1 cup whole milk
- 3/4 cup granulated sugar
- 1 cup dark chocolate, finely chopped
- 1 teaspoon vanilla extract
- 1/2 teaspoon ground chili powder (adjust to taste)
- Pinch of cayenne pepper (optional, for extra heat)

Instructions:

1. Prepare the Ice Cream Base:

    In a saucepan, combine the heavy cream, whole milk, and granulated sugar over medium heat.
    Stir the mixture until it begins to simmer, ensuring the sugar is completely dissolved.
    Once simmering, remove the saucepan from heat.

2. Add Chocolate:

    Add the finely chopped dark chocolate to the hot cream mixture. Stir until the chocolate is fully melted and incorporated.

3. Cool the Mixture:

    Allow the chocolate cream mixture to cool to room temperature.
    Cover the bowl and refrigerate for at least 4 hours or overnight to ensure it is thoroughly chilled.

4. Add Chili Heat:

    Once the mixture is chilled, stir in the vanilla extract, ground chili powder, and cayenne pepper (if using). Adjust the chili powder to your preferred level of heat.

5. Freeze in Ice Cream Maker:

    Pour the chilled Chocolate Chili Ice Cream mixture into your ice cream maker.
    Churn the mixture according to the manufacturer's instructions until it reaches a creamy ice cream consistency.

6. Transfer to Container:

Transfer the churned ice cream into a lidded container.

7. Final Freeze:

   Freeze the ice cream for an additional 2-4 hours or until it firms up to your preferred texture.

8. Scoop and Enjoy:

   Scoop the Chocolate Chili Ice Cream into bowls or cones.
   Savor the rich and spicy combination of chocolate and chili in each decadent spoonful.
   Serve and enjoy this bold and flavorful homemade frozen treat!

This Chocolate Chili Ice Cream offers a perfect balance of creamy chocolate sweetness and a subtle kick of chili heat. It's an adventurous and indulgent treat for those who appreciate a touch of spice in their desserts. Enjoy the unique flavor profile of this homemade ice cream!

Blackberry Basil Ice Cream

Ingredients:

- 2 cups fresh blackberries
- 1 cup granulated sugar
- 1 cup whole milk
- 2 cups heavy cream
- 1 teaspoon vanilla extract
- 1/2 cup fresh basil leaves, chopped

Instructions:

1. Prepare the Blackberry Puree:

    In a blender or food processor, puree the fresh blackberries until smooth.
    Strain the blackberry puree through a fine-mesh sieve to remove seeds. You can skip this step if you don't mind the seeds.

2. Infuse the Milk and Cream:

    In a saucepan, combine the whole milk and heavy cream over medium heat.
    Heat the mixture until it just begins to simmer, stirring occasionally.
    Remove the saucepan from heat and let it cool to room temperature.
    Stir in the vanilla extract.

3. Mix Blackberry Basil Base:

    In a large bowl, combine the blackberry puree and the cooled milk and cream mixture.
    Add the granulated sugar and mix until the sugar is fully dissolved.
    Stir in the chopped fresh basil leaves.

4. Chill the Mixture:

    Place the Blackberry Basil Ice Cream mixture in the refrigerator and let it chill for at least 4 hours or overnight to ensure it is thoroughly chilled.

5. Freeze in Ice Cream Maker:

    Pour the chilled blackberry basil mixture into your ice cream maker.

Churn the mixture according to the manufacturer's instructions until it reaches a creamy ice cream consistency.

6. Transfer to Container:

    Transfer the churned ice cream into a lidded container.

7. Final Freeze:

    Freeze the ice cream for an additional 2-4 hours or until it firms up to your preferred texture.

8. Scoop and Enjoy:

    Scoop the Blackberry Basil Ice Cream into bowls or cones.
    Savor the unique combination of sweet blackberries and aromatic basil in each luscious bite.
    Serve and relish this homemade frozen treat with a touch of summer freshness!

This Blackberry Basil Ice Cream brings together the sweetness of blackberries and the herbal notes of fresh basil, creating a refreshing and delightful frozen dessert. Enjoy the vibrant flavors of this homemade ice cream for a taste of summer in every scoop!

Peach Bourbon Ice Cream

Ingredients:

- 3 cups ripe peaches, peeled, pitted, and chopped
- 1 cup granulated sugar
- 1 tablespoon lemon juice
- 2 cups heavy cream
- 1 cup whole milk
- 1 teaspoon vanilla extract
- 1/4 cup bourbon (adjust to taste)

Instructions:

1. Prepare Peach Puree:

    In a blender or food processor, puree the ripe peaches until smooth.
    Stir in the lemon juice and set aside.

2. Infuse the Milk and Cream:

    In a saucepan, combine the heavy cream and whole milk over medium heat.
    Heat the mixture until it just begins to simmer, stirring occasionally.
    Remove the saucepan from heat and let it cool to room temperature.
    Stir in the vanilla extract and bourbon.

3. Mix Peach Bourbon Base:

    In a large bowl, combine the peach puree and the cooled milk and cream mixture.
    Add the granulated sugar and mix until the sugar is fully dissolved.

4. Chill the Mixture:

    Place the Peach Bourbon Ice Cream mixture in the refrigerator and let it chill for at least 4 hours or overnight to ensure it is thoroughly chilled.

5. Freeze in Ice Cream Maker:

    Pour the chilled peach bourbon mixture into your ice cream maker.
    Churn the mixture according to the manufacturer's instructions until it reaches a creamy ice cream consistency.

6. Transfer to Container:

Transfer the churned ice cream into a lidded container.

7. Final Freeze:

   Freeze the ice cream for an additional 2-4 hours or until it firms up to your preferred texture.

8. Scoop and Enjoy:

   Scoop the Peach Bourbon Ice Cream into bowls or cones.
   Revel in the sweet and boozy combination of ripe peaches and bourbon in every delicious bite.
   Serve and savor this homemade frozen treat with a touch of southern charm!

This Peach Bourbon Ice Cream is a delightful blend of fruity sweetness and the warmth of bourbon, making it a perfect treat for warm summer days or any occasion. Enjoy the rich and comforting flavors of this homemade ice cream!

Toasted Coconut Pineapple Ice Cream

Ingredients:

- 1 cup shredded coconut (sweetened or unsweetened)
- 2 cups heavy cream
- 1 cup whole milk
- 3/4 cup granulated sugar
- 1 teaspoon vanilla extract
- 1 cup crushed pineapple, well-drained
- 1/2 cup pineapple juice (from the drained crushed pineapple)

Instructions:

1. Toast Coconut:

    In a dry pan over medium heat, toast the shredded coconut until it turns golden brown and fragrant. Stir frequently to prevent burning.
    Once toasted, set aside a small portion for garnish and let the rest cool.

2. Infuse the Milk and Cream:

    In a saucepan, combine the heavy cream and whole milk over medium heat.
    Heat the mixture until it just begins to simmer, stirring occasionally.
    Remove the saucepan from heat and let it cool to room temperature.
    Stir in the vanilla extract.

3. Mix Toasted Coconut Base:

    In a large bowl, combine the cooled milk and cream mixture with the granulated sugar.
    Add the crushed pineapple and pineapple juice. Mix well.
    Stir in the majority of the toasted coconut, reserving some for garnish.

4. Chill the Mixture:

    Place the Toasted Coconut Pineapple Ice Cream mixture in the refrigerator and let it chill for at least 4 hours or overnight to ensure it is thoroughly chilled.

5. Freeze in Ice Cream Maker:

    Pour the chilled mixture into your ice cream maker.
    Churn the mixture according to the manufacturer's instructions until it reaches a creamy ice cream consistency.

6. Transfer to Container:

   Transfer the churned ice cream into a lidded container.

7. Final Freeze:

   Freeze the ice cream for an additional 2-4 hours or until it firms up to your preferred texture.

8. Scoop and Enjoy:

   Scoop the Toasted Coconut Pineapple Ice Cream into bowls or cones.
   Garnish with the reserved toasted coconut.
   Dive into the tropical paradise of flavors in every spoonful!

This Toasted Coconut Pineapple Ice Cream is a dreamy blend of tropical sweetness and nutty richness. It's the perfect frozen treat for warm days or anytime you crave a taste of the tropics. Enjoy the exotic flavors of this homemade ice cream!

Honey Roasted Fig Ice Cream

Ingredients:

- 1 pound fresh figs, stems removed and halved
- 1/4 cup honey
- 2 tablespoons brown sugar
- 2 cups heavy cream
- 1 cup whole milk
- 3/4 cup granulated sugar
- 1 teaspoon vanilla extract

Instructions:

1. Roast Figs:

    Preheat your oven to 400°F (200°C).
    Place the fig halves on a baking sheet and drizzle them with honey and brown sugar.
    Roast the figs in the preheated oven for about 15-20 minutes or until they are soft and caramelized. Let them cool.
    Once cooled, chop the roasted figs into smaller pieces.

2. Infuse the Milk and Cream:

    In a saucepan, combine the heavy cream and whole milk over medium heat.
    Heat the mixture until it just begins to simmer, stirring occasionally.
    Remove the saucepan from heat and let it cool to room temperature.
    Stir in the vanilla extract.

3. Mix Honey Roasted Fig Base:

    In a large bowl, combine the cooled milk and cream mixture with the granulated sugar.
    Add the chopped honey-roasted figs and mix well.

4. Chill the Mixture:

    Place the Honey Roasted Fig Ice Cream mixture in the refrigerator and let it chill for at least 4 hours or overnight to ensure it is thoroughly chilled.

5. Freeze in Ice Cream Maker:

Pour the chilled mixture into your ice cream maker.
Churn the mixture according to the manufacturer's instructions until it reaches a creamy ice cream consistency.

6. Transfer to Container:

    Transfer the churned ice cream into a lidded container.

7. Final Freeze:

    Freeze the ice cream for an additional 2-4 hours or until it firms up to your preferred texture.

8. Scoop and Enjoy:

    Scoop the Honey Roasted Fig Ice Cream into bowls or cones.
    Savor the decadent blend of honey-roasted figs in every delightful bite.
    Share and relish this exquisite homemade frozen treat!

This Honey Roasted Fig Ice Cream is a sophisticated and delightful dessert, perfect for those who appreciate the natural sweetness of figs combined with the richness of honey. Enjoy the luxurious flavors of this homemade ice cream!

Brown Butter Maple Pecan Ice Cream

Ingredients:

- 1 cup pecans, chopped
- 1/2 cup unsalted butter
- 2 cups heavy cream
- 1 cup whole milk
- 3/4 cup brown sugar, packed
- 1/4 cup pure maple syrup
- 1 teaspoon vanilla extract
- 1/4 teaspoon salt

Instructions:

1. Toast Pecans:

    In a dry pan over medium heat, toast the chopped pecans until they become fragrant and lightly browned. Stir frequently to prevent burning. Set aside to cool.

2. Brown Butter:

    In a separate saucepan, melt the unsalted butter over medium heat.
    Once melted, continue to cook the butter until it turns golden brown with a nutty aroma.
    Be attentive to prevent burning.
    Remove the browned butter from heat and let it cool.

3. Infuse the Milk and Cream:

    In a saucepan, combine the heavy cream and whole milk over medium heat.
    Heat the mixture until it just begins to simmer, stirring occasionally.
    Remove the saucepan from heat and let it cool to room temperature.
    Stir in the vanilla extract and a pinch of salt.

4. Mix Brown Butter Maple Pecan Base:

    In a large bowl, combine the cooled milk and cream mixture with the brown sugar.
    Slowly whisk in the browned butter and maple syrup until the sugar is fully dissolved.
    Add the toasted pecans and mix well.

5. Chill the Mixture:

Place the Brown Butter Maple Pecan Ice Cream mixture in the refrigerator and let it chill for at least 4 hours or overnight to ensure it is thoroughly chilled.

6. Freeze in Ice Cream Maker:

    Pour the chilled mixture into your ice cream maker.
    Churn the mixture according to the manufacturer's instructions until it reaches a creamy ice cream consistency.

7. Transfer to Container:

    Transfer the churned ice cream into a lidded container.

8. Final Freeze:

    Freeze the ice cream for an additional 2-4 hours or until it firms up to your preferred texture.

9. Scoop and Enjoy:

    Scoop the Brown Butter Maple Pecan Ice Cream into bowls or cones.
    Delight in the rich, nutty, and maple-infused flavors in every scoop.
    Share and savor this indulgent homemade frozen treat!

This Brown Butter Maple Pecan Ice Cream is a perfect blend of warmth from brown butter, sweetness from maple syrup, and crunch from toasted pecans. Enjoy the comforting and luxurious flavors of this homemade ice cream!

Strawberry Balsamic Swirl Ice Cream

Ingredients:

- 2 cups fresh strawberries, hulled and sliced
- 1/2 cup granulated sugar
- 2 tablespoons balsamic vinegar
- 2 cups heavy cream
- 1 cup whole milk
- 3/4 cup granulated sugar
- 1 teaspoon vanilla extract

Instructions:

1. Prepare Strawberry Balsamic Swirl:

    In a blender or food processor, puree the fresh strawberries with 1/2 cup of sugar until smooth.
    Pour the strawberry puree into a saucepan and heat over medium heat.
    Stir in the balsamic vinegar and cook the mixture until it thickens slightly, about 5-7 minutes.
    Remove from heat and let the strawberry balsamic swirl mixture cool. Once cooled, place it in the refrigerator to chill.

2. Infuse the Milk and Cream:

    In a separate saucepan, combine the heavy cream and whole milk over medium heat.
    Heat the mixture until it just begins to simmer, stirring occasionally.
    Remove the saucepan from heat and let it cool to room temperature.
    Stir in the vanilla extract.

3. Mix Strawberry Balsamic Swirl Base:

    In a large bowl, combine the cooled milk and cream mixture with 3/4 cup of granulated sugar.
    Pour the mixture into your ice cream maker.
    Churn the mixture according to the manufacturer's instructions until it reaches a creamy ice cream consistency.

4. Swirl the Balsamic Mixture:

    Transfer the churned ice cream into a lidded container.
    Spoon dollops of the chilled strawberry balsamic swirl over the ice cream.

Use a knife or spatula to gently swirl the balsamic mixture into the ice cream, creating a marbled effect.

5. Final Freeze:

   Freeze the ice cream for an additional 2-4 hours or until it firms up to your preferred texture.

6. Scoop and Enjoy:

   Scoop the Strawberry Balsamic Swirl Ice Cream into bowls or cones.
   Relish the sweet and tangy combination in every delightful bite.
   Share and savor this unique and sophisticated homemade frozen treat!

This Strawberry Balsamic Swirl Ice Cream offers a perfect balance of sweetness and acidity, making it a refreshing and indulgent dessert option. Enjoy the vibrant flavors of this homemade ice cream!

Chai Tea Latte Ice Cream

Ingredients:

Chai Base:

- 2 cups whole milk
- 2 cups heavy cream
- 1/2 cup loose-leaf black tea or 6-8 chai tea bags
- 1 cinnamon stick
- 4-6 cardamom pods, lightly crushed
- 4-6 whole cloves
- 1-2 star anise
- 1 teaspoon ground ginger
- 1/2 teaspoon ground nutmeg
- 1/2 cup granulated sugar
- 1/4 cup honey or maple syrup
- 1 teaspoon vanilla extract
- Pinch of salt

Instructions:

1. Infuse Chai Base:

　　In a saucepan, combine the whole milk and heavy cream over medium heat.
　　Add the loose-leaf black tea or chai tea bags, cinnamon stick, crushed cardamom pods, whole cloves, star anise, ground ginger, and ground nutmeg.
　　Heat the mixture until it just begins to simmer. Allow it to simmer for about 5 minutes, stirring occasionally.
　　Remove the saucepan from heat, cover it, and let the chai mixture steep for an additional 15-20 minutes to infuse the flavors.
　　Strain the chai mixture to remove the tea leaves or tea bags and the whole spices.

2. Mix Chai Tea Latte Ice Cream Base:

　　In a clean saucepan, combine the strained chai-infused milk and cream with granulated sugar, honey or maple syrup, vanilla extract, and a pinch of salt.
　　Heat the mixture over medium heat until it just begins to simmer, stirring to dissolve the sugar.
　　Remove the saucepan from heat and let the chai tea latte base cool to room temperature.

3. Chill the Mixture:

   Once cooled, refrigerate the chai tea latte ice cream base for at least 4 hours or overnight to ensure it is thoroughly chilled.

4. Freeze in Ice Cream Maker:

   Pour the chilled mixture into your ice cream maker.
   Churn the mixture according to the manufacturer's instructions until it reaches a creamy ice cream consistency.

5. Transfer to Container:

   Transfer the churned ice cream into a lidded container.

6. Final Freeze:

   Freeze the ice cream for an additional 2-4 hours or until it firms up to your preferred texture.

7. Scoop and Enjoy:

   Scoop the Chai Tea Latte Ice Cream into bowls or cones.
   Savor the rich and aromatic flavors of chai in every luscious bite.
   Share and relish this comforting and unique homemade frozen treat!

This Chai Tea Latte Ice Cream is a wonderful blend of warming spices and the richness of black tea. Enjoy the cozy and comforting experience of your favorite chai tea transformed into a delicious frozen dessert!

Peanut Butter and Jelly Ice Cream

Ingredients:

Peanut Butter Ice Cream Base:

- 2 cups heavy cream
- 1 cup whole milk
- 3/4 cup granulated sugar
- 1/2 cup creamy peanut butter
- 1 teaspoon vanilla extract
- Pinch of salt

Jelly Swirl:

- 1/2 cup your favorite fruit jam or jelly (strawberry, raspberry, grape, etc.)

Instructions:

1. Prepare Peanut Butter Ice Cream Base:

    In a saucepan, combine the heavy cream and whole milk over medium heat.
    Heat the mixture until it just begins to simmer, stirring occasionally.
    In a separate bowl, whisk together granulated sugar, creamy peanut butter, vanilla extract, and a pinch of salt until well combined.
    Slowly whisk the peanut butter mixture into the heated milk and cream until smooth.
    Continue heating and stirring until the mixture is well-blended and just begins to simmer.
    Remove the saucepan from heat and let the peanut butter ice cream base cool to room temperature.

2. Chill the Mixture:

    Once cooled, refrigerate the peanut butter ice cream base for at least 4 hours or overnight to ensure it is thoroughly chilled.

3. Freeze in Ice Cream Maker:

    Pour the chilled peanut butter ice cream base into your ice cream maker.
    Churn the mixture according to the manufacturer's instructions until it reaches a creamy ice cream consistency.

4. Prepare Jelly Swirl:

   In a small saucepan, gently heat the fruit jam or jelly over low heat until it becomes more fluid. Let it cool.

5. Swirl the Jelly into Ice Cream:

   Transfer the churned ice cream into a lidded container.
   Spoon dollops of the cooled fruit jam or jelly over the ice cream.
   Use a knife or spatula to gently swirl the jelly into the ice cream, creating a marbled effect.

6. Final Freeze:

   Freeze the peanut butter and jelly ice cream for an additional 2-4 hours or until it firms up to your preferred texture.

7. Scoop and Enjoy:

   Scoop the Peanut Butter and Jelly Ice Cream into bowls or cones.
   Savor the nostalgic and delicious combination of peanut butter and jelly in every creamy bite.
   Share and relish this classic homemade frozen treat!

This Peanut Butter and Jelly Ice Cream brings together the timeless flavors of childhood in a cool and creamy dessert. Enjoy the perfect blend of nutty peanut butter and fruity jam in this delightful homemade ice cream!

Rum Raisin Ice Cream

Ingredients:

- 1 cup raisins
- 1/2 cup dark rum
- 2 cups heavy cream
- 1 cup whole milk
- 3/4 cup granulated sugar
- 4 large egg yolks
- 1 teaspoon vanilla extract
- Pinch of salt

Instructions:

1. Soak Raisins in Rum:

    Place the raisins in a small bowl and pour the dark rum over them.
    Let the raisins soak in the rum for at least 1-2 hours, allowing them to plump up and absorb the flavor.

2. Prepare Rum Raisin Ice Cream Base:

    In a saucepan, combine the heavy cream and whole milk over medium heat.
    Heat the mixture until it just begins to simmer, stirring occasionally.
    In a separate bowl, whisk together granulated sugar, egg yolks, vanilla extract, and a pinch of salt until well combined.
    Slowly whisk the egg yolk mixture into the heated milk and cream until smooth.
    Continue heating and stirring until the mixture thickens and coats the back of a spoon. Do not let it boil.
    Remove the saucepan from heat and let the rum raisin ice cream base cool to room temperature.

3. Chill the Mixture:

    Once cooled, refrigerate the rum raisin ice cream base for at least 4 hours or overnight to ensure it is thoroughly chilled.

4. Freeze in Ice Cream Maker:

    Strain the raisins from the rum, reserving the rum for later.
    Pour the chilled rum raisin ice cream base into your ice cream maker.

Churn the mixture according to the manufacturer's instructions until it reaches a creamy ice cream consistency.

5. Add Raisins and Rum:

    During the last few minutes of churning, add the plumped raisins to the ice cream. Pour in a little bit of the reserved rum as well for an extra burst of flavor. Adjust according to your taste preference.

6. Transfer to Container:

    Transfer the churned rum raisin ice cream into a lidded container.

7. Final Freeze:

    Freeze the ice cream for an additional 2-4 hours or until it firms up to your preferred texture.

8. Scoop and Enjoy:

    Scoop the Rum Raisin Ice Cream into bowls or cones.
    Delight in the luxurious and boozy flavor of rum-soaked raisins in every creamy bite.
    Share and savor this sophisticated homemade frozen treat!

This Rum Raisin Ice Cream is a perfect blend of creamy richness and the warmth of rum-infused raisins. Enjoy the indulgent and grown-up flavor of this delightful homemade frozen dessert!

Lavender Blueberry Cheesecake Ice Cream

Ingredients:

Blueberry Swirl:

- 1 cup fresh or frozen blueberries
- 1/4 cup granulated sugar
- 1 tablespoon lemon juice

Lavender Base:

- 2 cups heavy cream
- 1 cup whole milk
- 3/4 cup granulated sugar
- 2 tablespoons dried culinary lavender (make sure it's food-grade)
- 4 ounces cream cheese, softened
- 1 teaspoon vanilla extract
- Pinch of salt

Instructions:

1. Prepare Blueberry Swirl:

   In a small saucepan, combine blueberries, granulated sugar, and lemon juice. Cook over medium heat, stirring occasionally, until the blueberries break down and the mixture thickens slightly (about 10-15 minutes).
   Remove from heat and let it cool. You can strain out the blueberry skins if desired for a smoother swirl.

2. Infuse Lavender Base:

   In a saucepan, combine the heavy cream and whole milk over medium heat.
   Add dried culinary lavender to the milk and cream mixture.
   Heat the mixture until it just begins to simmer. Allow it to simmer for about 5 minutes, stirring occasionally.
   Remove the saucepan from heat and let the lavender steep for an additional 15-20 minutes.
   Strain out the lavender from the mixture.

3. Make Lavender Cheesecake Base:

In a bowl, whisk together the softened cream cheese, granulated sugar, vanilla extract, and a pinch of salt until smooth.
Gradually whisk the lavender-infused milk and cream into the cream cheese mixture until well combined.
Let the lavender cheesecake base cool to room temperature.

4. Chill the Mixture:

   Once cooled, refrigerate the lavender cheesecake ice cream base for at least 4 hours or overnight to ensure it is thoroughly chilled.

5. Freeze in Ice Cream Maker:

   Pour the chilled lavender cheesecake ice cream base into your ice cream maker. Churn the mixture according to the manufacturer's instructions until it reaches a creamy ice cream consistency.

6. Swirl in Blueberry Mixture:

   Transfer the churned ice cream into a lidded container.
   Spoon dollops of the cooled blueberry swirl over the ice cream.
   Use a knife or spatula to gently swirl the blueberry mixture into the ice cream, creating a marbled effect.

7. Final Freeze:

   Freeze the Lavender Blueberry Cheesecake Ice Cream for an additional 2-4 hours or until it firms up to your preferred texture.

8. Scoop and Enjoy:

   Scoop the Lavender Blueberry Cheesecake Ice Cream into bowls or cones.
   Relish the unique and sophisticated flavor combination in every luscious bite.
   Share and savor this homemade frozen treat that combines the floral notes of lavender, the sweetness of blueberries, and the richness of cheesecake!

This Lavender Blueberry Cheesecake Ice Cream is a perfect way to enjoy a sophisticated and refreshing dessert with a unique twist. Enjoy the delicate flavors and creamy texture in each delightful scoop!

Coconut Lime Mojito Sorbet

Ingredients:

- 1 cup coconut milk
- 1 cup water
- 3/4 cup granulated sugar
- Zest of 2 limes
- 1/2 cup fresh lime juice (about 4-5 limes)
- 2 tablespoons fresh mint leaves, chopped
- 2 tablespoons white rum (optional, for an adult version)
- Toasted coconut flakes for garnish (optional)
- Lime slices and mint sprigs for garnish (optional)

Instructions:

1. Make Simple Syrup:

    In a saucepan, combine water and granulated sugar over medium heat.
    Stir until the sugar dissolves, and the mixture comes to a simmer. Simmer for 2-3 minutes to create a simple syrup.
    Remove from heat and let it cool to room temperature.

2. Prepare Coconut Lime Base:

    In a mixing bowl, combine coconut milk, lime zest, lime juice, chopped mint leaves, and the cooled simple syrup.
    Optionally, add white rum for an adult version and stir well.

3. Chill the Mixture:

    Cover the coconut lime mixture and refrigerate for at least 2-4 hours, allowing the flavors to meld.

4. Freeze in Sorbet Maker:

    Pour the chilled coconut lime mojito sorbet mixture into your sorbet maker.
    Churn the mixture according to the manufacturer's instructions until it reaches a sorbet-like consistency.

5. Final Freeze:

Transfer the churned sorbet into a lidded container.
Freeze for an additional 2-4 hours or until it reaches your desired firmness.

6. Serve and Garnish:

Scoop the Coconut Lime Mojito Sorbet into bowls or cones.
Garnish with toasted coconut flakes, lime slices, and mint sprigs if desired.
Enjoy the refreshing combination of coconut, lime, and mint in this tropical sorbet!

This Coconut Lime Mojito Sorbet is a perfect way to cool off on a hot day with a taste of the tropics. Whether you're enjoying it by the pool or as a delightful dessert, savor the zesty and minty goodness in every spoonful!

www.ingramcontent.com/pod-product-compliance
Lightning Source LLC
LaVergne TN
LVHW081555060526
838201LV00054B/1904